# A Voice Unstilled

## Archbishop Ndingi Mwana 'a Nzeki

Waithaka Waihenya
Fr Ndikaru wa Teresia

An imprint of

PUBLISHERS
expanding minds

Published by **Sasa Sema** Publications
*An imprint of Longhorn Publishers*

Longhorn Kenya Ltd.,
Funzi Road, Industrial Area,
P.O. Box 18033-00500,
Nairobi, Kenya.

Longhorn Uganda Ltd.,
Plot 731, Kamwokya Area,
Mawanda Road, P.O. Box 24745,
Kampala, Uganda.

Longhorn Publishers (T) Ltd.,
Kinondoni Plot No.4
Block 37B
Kawawa Road
Dar es Salaam, Tanzania.

© Waithaka Waihenya & Fr Ndikaru wa Teresia 2009

All rights reserved. No part of this publication may be reproduced, stored in a retrieval system or transmitted in any form or by any means, electronic, mechanical, photocopying, recording or otherwise without the prior written permission of the copyright owner.

First published 2009

Cover design by Longhorn Publishers

**ISBN 978 9966 36 511 7**

Printed by Printwell Ltd., Road A, Off Enterprise Road, Industrial Area, P.O. Box 5216-00506, Nairobi, Kenya.

# TABLE OF CONTENTS

1. Should I congratulate or sympathise with you?...............1
2. I will call you Mwana 'a Nzeki ...............9
3. In the seminary ...............20
4. The big day ...............25
5. A priest among white missionaries ...............35
6. Education and a handy ally ...............46
7. First black bishop of Machakos ...............53
8. Home in Machakos ...............58
9. Into a political hotbed ...............67
10. Tempest in the Rift Valley ...............84
11. In the eye of the storm ...............104
12. Oh, another Pope is here ...............135
13. Culture shock ...............153
14. Reconstructing the African face of Christ ...............169
15. The thorny issue of celibacy ...............179
16. Fighting the culture of death ...............192
17. Serving three presidents ...............197
    Epilogue ...............209
    List of Latin terms used ...............212
    Pictorial appendix ...............213
    Index ...............221

# PREFACE

In faithfulness to the Great Commission, a young man deep in the Kenyan hinterland responded to the call to serve as a priest of God in the Roman Catholic Church. This young man was Ndingi Mwana 'a Nzeki. This was unsettling, not because of the uncompromising message of Jesus Christ, but most of all that the Church he gave his life to was propagated by humans with a tendency to err.

The old adage "the truth sets you free but first it makes you miserable" must have rung true in the life of Archbishop Ndingi as he sought to live what he believed. A man of great faith and character, the story of the Catholic Church in Kenya cannot be complete without the chapter on this tenacious crusader for justice and peace.

The retired Archbishop Emeritus R.S. Ndingi Mwana 'a Nzeki, has been and continues to be a voice of faith, justice and peace. Growing up without the benefit of a Christian family background, the story of His Grace is and will be for many a source of inspiration and a model of life lived as 'the salt of the earth'. A man of small physical stature, he distinguished himself as a giant in his clamour for justice and peace, especially for the poor and voiceless. Always a faithful son of the Roman Catholic Church, he based his pronouncements on the social teachings of the Church, sometimes earning the label 'radical' as he sought to champion the people's rights in Kenya and in the Church.

With a distinct tendency to lose his temper in the face of perceived or real ineptitude, a peek into the heart of this man of God reveals a deeply caring man, a fact that endeared him to those with whom he worked and especially the clergy who he had to lead, correct and inspire. A man of deep prayer, constancy and faithfulness in spiritual matters, he berated the sinner for his sin while holding out his hand in forgiveness, perhaps aware of his own failings despite his good intentions.

At a time when religious bodies are being accused of having lost their sting as the conscience of the nation, Archbishop Ndingi is held up as the image of the courageous crusader for justice and peace. He is to be emulated and remembered for the inspirational story of his life.

While the fight for peace and justice continues, many have benefited from the efforts of the gallant men and women who, like Archbishop Ndingi put their lives on the line to make pronouncements that chipped away at the edifices of evil.

That the archbishop was entrusted with leading the resettlement programme for those displaced during the post-election violence of 2008/2009 is testament to the trust and high esteem this man of God is held in. It is not unexpected that the archbishop continues to lead an active life on behalf of the victims of injustice, even in retirement.

Fr Patrick Kanja Wachira

Chaplain, University of Nairobi

# FOREWORD

In the course of life, you often meet people who distinguish themselves in a way that makes you admire them forever. It may be because of their character, achievement, determination or something so monumental that they have done in their lives that their memory lives on forever in the minds of those who meet them.

I met His Grace Raphael Ndingi Mwana 'a Nzeki when we were beginning our pastoral lives in the seminary decades ago. From the word go, there was something distinctive in the man, or so I thought. Today, when I look at his life, I get vindicated by that early feeling I got about him.

The Emeritus Archbishop of Nairobi has laboured faithfully in the Lord's vineyard since his ordination to priesthood on 1st January 1961. It is a long road he has travelled. But it is also one that is marked by some remarkable achievements.

Often, it is improper to eulogise a man while he is still alive. But to write a foreword about Ndingi's life behoves one to paint a picture of the man and his character as faithfully as he has lived his life.

His track record as a priest of the Archdiocese of Nairobi, as Bishop of Machakos and later Nakuru diocese and finally as the archbishop of Nairobi speaks for itself. As this book amply outlines, he served as bishop in some of the most tumultuous years of this nation's history. He was in Machakos when the Church was just beginning to take root and when African priests were just beginning to minister to their peoples. While in Nakuru, the infamous ethnic clashes in the Rift Valley took place in 1992. This was a period that demanded that a true man of God rise up to defend what was right. Ndingi, as this book outlines, faithfully and unfailingly rose up to defend the rights of the people. This was at a time when the Moi regime was feared, when no one, other than the bravest, could dare question it. But Ndingi did and the rest is history.

Besides knowing him as a co-worker when we both served as priests at Our Lady of Visitation, Makadara, Nairobi in the 1960s and later as bishops in the Kenya Episcopal Conference, I have come to treasure him as a personal friend. He is now retired but certainly not tired. I preceded him in retirement and I fondly remember how he welcomed me to Nairobi and contributed to the building of my retirement house at the Queen of Apostles Seminary.

When I look back on his life, I see a man who not only harbours a great thirst for justice but who also nurtures courage as a virtue to be emulated by all those who wish to stand for truth and justice in their pastoral ministries.

This book is not just a story of a man of God. It is a study in what virtue and courage can do for humanity. It is a celebration of a life well lived and a service magnificently offered to the people of God. I hope all who read it will be as edified as I am by the life of this great man of God.

+ Most Reverend John Njenga
Emeritus Archbishop of Mombasa
28th August 2008
St Augustine of Hippo

# ACKNOWLEDGEMENTS

There are those people without whom this book would never have been written, or even if it had, would not have appeared in the form it does. We would therefore like to thank Fr Patrick Wachira Kanja, the chaplain of the University of Nairobi who offered handy insight into the life of Archbishop Ndingi under whom he served in two dioceses: Nakuru and Nairobi.

Fr Francis Mirango was Ndingi's procurator in Nakuru and thus knew and understood the bishop in a way few others did. We thank him for his openness and availability for interviews in the course of writing this book.

Fr Joseph M'lengera shared with us much of what appears in this book. Peter Mbuchi Metho now a layman, Fr Dennis Newman and Fr P.J. McCamphill, Fr Moses Muraya, Vicar General, and Fr Peter Mungai of Nakuru Diocese also gave us helpful insights. We feel indebted to Fr James Maloba, Ndingi's long time personal assistant, for arranging interviews with the bishop and Fr Peter Kimani who encouraged us to write.

Archbishop John Njenga, Bishop Emeritus of Mombasa, provided a window through which we were able to steal a glimpse into the life of Ndingi. Shortly before his death, Archbishop Nicodemus Kirima shared with us his thoughts about the bishop. We thank him posthumously.

Fr Lawrence Njoroge, the chaplain of Jomo Kenyatta University of Agriculture and Technology, kindly read through the manuscript and made useful suggestions. Samson Mwangi and Sister Angelina Mumbi, Ndingi's driver and secretary respectively, contributed immensely to the writing of this book.

Though the subject of this book, we would like to thank Archbishop Ndingi for being available for interminable interviews and for giving us access to his private diaries and documents.

# CHAPTER ONE

## *Should I congratulate or sympathise with you?*

It was his greatest day of joy. As a newly ordained Bishop, the young priest reveled in the adulation of the enthusiastic crowd now milling around him and which wanted to kiss the Episcopal ring that had just been slipped into his right hand finger by Pope Paul VI.

He welcomed their curiosity with humility, their adulation with a touch of bewilderment. Some fixed their gaze on the pectoral cross that hang on his chest while others admired the new vestments that the newly consecrated bishop was adorned in.

He waved at the crowd as he pondered about his new mission and the path he had travelled to the episcopacy. For some minutes, he allowed his mind to travel the road he had taken opening a zone at the back of his mind where history was replayed in dazzling technicolour.

It had been a long and almost treacherous road. He had endured a lot and in his own way, achieved a lot. He had been to the lowest valleys and climbed heart-wrenching mountains but amidst all that, he had kept the faith. Now he was here in the sweltering heat of Kampala, Uganda, on this morning of June 3, 1969, receiving the one red hat, the zucchetto, that so many priests aspire for but so few get. He unleashed his mind to wonder unhindered through that unwinding road that had finally belched him onto the shores of episcopacy.

His days at the seminary were worth remembering. He had come a long way from the deeper parts of Kambaland in Eastern Kenya and lived out his heart's desire almost unfettered. He had chosen a life not many in his generation could even contemplate: priesthood. Despite his fortitude, there were days at the seminary when life was just too hard for Raphael Ndingi Mwana 'a Nzeki.

This was at a time when the Church in Kenya was dominated by the missionaries. Nairobi Archdiocese, an expansive zone stretching all the way to Kambaland then, was under Archbishop J. J. McCarthy, a white missionary. Many others were of this ilk. The thought of an African bishop had just a year before, been unthinkable. Even the white priest could not contemplate it. They made snide remarks about what would happen at the possibility of an African being made bishop. Some did not hide the fact that they would quit the Church altogether.

"If an African becomes bishop, I will quit," some vowed. It was a cheeky thing to say for any priest, for even though sometimes said in jest, it showed how lowly some white priests regarded their African counterparts.

Still, Ndingi had chosen to walk on a road less travelled, starting from his homeland in Mwala to Kilimambogo, Moshi and Kiserian seminaries. Here, he had lived out his faith, climbed a few spiritual valleys, plunged into some lowly depths, experienced challenges and variously overcame them. He remembered the days when he had to go through what St John of the Cross called 'the dark night of the soul' and how fervently he had prayed for deliverance.

## Should I congratulate or sympathise with you?

Since memory is the penalty we pay for existence, there was no way to escape it even for Ndingi, resplendent with new bishopric vestments now dazzling in the sweltering heat of the Ugandan capital. As he stood acknowledging cheers and congratulations, torments of his memory took him back to that distant day when he almost quit the seminary. Had he done so, the course of his life would have been remarkably different. That day was to inform his life in a most seminal manner.

This was at Kiserian Seminary, about 20 kilometres from the city of Nairobi. The seminary could only be built in the outskirts because the city was in the area generally referred to as 'the White Highlands.' White settlers who dominated the area had carved out huge pieces of land for themselves and lived in profligate luxury, unperturbed by the chaotic world of the natives around them. But Kiserian was virtually virgin land. The population was scanty and much of the wide expanse was inhabited by wild animals. Only a small patch was developed. The area lacked infrastructure and there were no amenities such as those one would find in the city.

The seminary was built of timber, exotically polished with oil so as to keep away the rapacity of ants. It nestled in a basin between two hills. From afar, it looked like a haven in the bush for it was planted right in the middle of an animal infested wilderness. At night, this place was unbelievably cold. Some seminarians called it Siberia, while others regarded the stay in the place as the penalty they had to pay for choosing to serve the Lord. The place was so heavily infested with mosquitoes that some seminarians joked that the mosquitoes had been specially poured into the valley by the Devil to dissuade them from accomplishing their priestly mission. Sadly, there were no mosquito nets to shield the young seminarians from the viscious mosquito bites; health care was virtually non-existent. If one scratched the bites, they would immediately swell, developing welts that made one resemble a victim of a scabrous disease.

But none of the seminarians was complaining. They believed that suffering was God-ordained and complaining unprovidential. They also believed that they would overcome this minor obstacle on the way to their own Calvary. In their own peculiar philosophy, they bore their cross with fortitude, believing that there would be hefty rewards at the final Golgotha.

However, there was also another side to that coin. The seminarians were afraid of making their complaints public because the Father rector, Fr Sean Grogan, was one harsh and strict man who lived in austerity; a ruthless disciplinarian who expected the seminarians to grin and bear all the sufferings visited on them stoically. Some said that he could not distinguish between suffering and enforcement of discipline.

The Father rector would make the students walk on foot all the way from Nairobi to Kiserian through Ongata Rongai, a long tedious journey. This was an expansive wilderness then which still forms a good part of the Nairobi National Park today. In this peril, the students would walk, hoping not to come across lions on the hunt. This, however, did not in anyway bother the rector.

At times, the rector would go away with the keys to the store, plunging the whole institution into pangs of prolonged hunger. It would have been easier to explain that the rector did this on racial grounds; that he wanted to punish the black students, but there were many Irish students also who suffered the same fate when Fr Grogan went away with the keys or engaged in one of his unbelievable acts of meanness.

## Should I congratulate or sympathise with you?

This habit of plunging the whole institution into hunger was one of his most egregious acts of meanness and it affected some students for many years afterwards. Archbishop John Njenga, the Archbishop Emeritus of Mombasa, who was in the same class with Ndingi, cannot stand the sight of a bunch of keys today. If keys could make them starve then, he now says, he has no desire to see them ever. He does not lock any room in the house to which he retired in the outskirts of the city of Nairobi.

Despite the extremes of the weather, Fr Grogan made the students dig quarries. The seminarians developed calloused hands and aching joints but Fr Grogan was unflinching. He would use cruel language on the students; language which those who were present say would have no place in a seminary today. There was no doubt that Africans got the sharper end of the stick but everyone else also suffered under the sadistic reign of this rector.

One day during the Holy Week, young Ndingi developed a severe pain in the hip joint. "It was so severe I could hardly walk," he remembers, many years later. He brought this to the attention of the rector expecting some sympathy and, at best, some solution. Unfortunately, the response was unbelievable. The rector looked at Ndingi and shouted, "bend!"

Ndingi stared in disbelief and shock at the rector's instructions. He could barely walk, lie down or even sit, and the priest was asking him to bend. He looked at the priest and surmised that the rector just wanted to punish him. "Bend!" the priest barked again. It was a voice that brooked no room for argument. It reverberated against the stillness of the valley and assaulted the ears of all those who were feeling the pain alongside young Ndingi at that moment. The young seminarian was astonished.

"I cannot bend," he responded, steeling his nerves against that assault and choosing to stand his ground rather than make worse the excruciating pain of the aching joint. The priest glowered at him. The seminarian and the priest were locked in a silent confrontation like two buffaloes, peering into each other's eye and waiting for the other to flinch. No other word was spoken between the two. After a while, Ndingi ambled away in pain and was deeply saddened that he had been completely abandoned in his agony. He looked back and saw the nonchalant priest walking away, completely unperturbed by Ndingi's plight and perhaps unbothered by the near confrontation that had ensued.

That night, Ndingi decided that he had had enough. He was the Head Prefect and he could see the silent suffering of his fellow seminarians who were too timid and too cowed to approach the priest whenever they had a problem that required his attention.

Ndingi thought about the rector as he lay nursing his painful joint and looking at the trusses of the roof. He made one resolve. He would write the rector a no-holds-barred letter explaining exactly what was wrong in the seminary and pointing out those responsible. If he got expelled for it, he would be ready to take the consequences. After all, he was a trained teacher and his level of education allowed him to join the police force: his other heart's desire.

He set out to write the letter, outlining the inhuman conditions in the seminary and the tough life there. He mentioned episodes when the rector had tried the resolve of the seminarians and suggested that the Fr rector change his approach to governance.

## Should I congratulate or sympathise with you?

When the priest got the letter, he was livid. He sent for Ndingi. Unafraid, the seminarian heeded the summons and headed straight to the office of the rector where he knew his fate would be sealed. He found him holding the letter, red in the face, eyes emitting fire. He was waving the letter like a fan against his face.

"Did you write this letter?" he demanded.

"Yes, I wrote it," Ndingi responded, unable to mask the bravery that was welled up in him begging to be belched out.

"What do you want to say?" the rector growled.

"It's all in the letter," he responded. "I hope you have read it all."

Ndingi had made one resolve: that he would take whatever the consequences this particular episode invited. He was ready to leave the seminary and he well knew that this would perhaps be the most probable outcome of his action. But if it came to that, he knew those who remained would at least benefit from the likely changes occasioned by his letter.

Realising that the young man was determined to stand by what he had written, the rector flinched. He dropped the letter on his desk and turned away. Ndingi walked away, unsure if he had escaped the guillotine. He walked back to the dormitory contemplating how close he had come to quitting the seminary. No one spoke about that letter again and none of the grievances he had raised were ever addressed.

Much later, Ndingi burned the letter because, on rereading it, he realised it was too harsh. He had kept the letter so that it could serve as evidence if the need arose or in case he got discontinued. Now that he had overcome that hurdle, there was no need to keep the letter.

As these thoughts fleeted across his mind, he saw a tall lanky figure approach him. The man's visage was unmistakable. It was the harsh rector. He proffered his hand and Ndingi shook it. The two men looked at each other.

"Should I congratulate you or sympathise with you?" he asked.

Ndingi paused and replied, "Do both."

With that, the newly ordained bishop took on a new path that would lead him to strange, exciting territories.

## CHAPTER TWO

## *I will call you Mwana'a Nzeki*

Machakos is a dry, almost semi–arid and somewhat hilly place. In the best of days, the scene is breathtaking with undulating hills spreading to as far as the eye can see. Machakos was established in 1889, ten years before Nairobi and was the first administrative centre for the British colony in Kenya.

However, in 1899, the colonialists moved the capital to Nairobi since Machakos by-passed the Kenya-Uganda Railway line that was under construction. The town and the district were named after Masaku, a Kamba chief whose name is still mentioned in awe to this day.

It was in Machakos that Raphael Ndingi was born, in the division of Mwala. The Holy Ghost priest who baptised the young man in 1945, Father Edward Fitz, wrote on the birth certificate that he was born in 1931.

Ndingi has no reason to dispute this but he has no compelling reason to take it as the gospel truth either. Then as it is now, the Church kept all the records and, invariably, acted as the barometer for the villages within their working boundaries. At Kabaa Mission in Machakos where Ndingi was baptised, the Holy Ghost Fathers had established an almost unassailable foothold, representing to the locals the unseen face of God, His will and presence. They were believed totally by the villagers and they had attained an infallibility that made them get away with anything. They had come from far to evangelise Africa and had brought with them their schools, the Church and medical facilities. The locals adored them.

The fifth born child of Joseph Nzeki Ngila, a blacksmith, and Maria Muthoki, Ndingi grew up in a close-knit family. His father was a polygamist. Between Ndingi and the third born was his sister Katunge, who was named after another sibling who had passed on. Katunge in Akamba means replacing one who has died. Ndingi grew up without knowing the identity of the one who had died and together with his three sisters and one brother, they made up the Nzeki family. Though starting out as non-Christians, the family was later to become fiercely Christian and implacably Catholic. It was no wonder then that there was another person who was pivotal in the Nzeki family. This was a priest in Machakos named Fr Jim Kavanagh who had become so familiar with the Christians of his parish that he was a part of every clan and every ridge of every village.

Over time, young Ndingi came to like the priest by dint of his frequent visits to the parish and the two grew fiercely fond of each other. Years later when he became a priest, Fr Kavanagh looked at the young man and told him, "Raphael, son of Nzeki, I will now be calling you Mwana 'a Nzeki." Ndingi liked the name especially because it also denoted his African roots. From that day, Ndingi adopted the name Mwana 'a Nzeki and it is by this name that he became known as a priest and by which he is known up to this day.

In the 1930s, the missionaries were trying to popularise schooling in Machakos but the locals were still holding onto their traditional ways. In 1937, they established a primary school, Myanyani Primary School, which was only a kilometre away from Ndingi's parents' home. There was a tradition among chiefs in that region that required a parent with two or three boys to send at least one to school. Ndingi's unbaptised elder brother, Kamulo Nzeki, was sent to school in 1940. Unfortunately, he dropped off at Standard Three. When it came to the sub-chief's attention that none of Nzeki's sons was in school, he sent a message to the chief complaining that Nzeki had not sent any son to school as was required by the chieftainship.

If parents failed to heed the chief's warning to send one of their sons to school, they had to give a cow to the chief for him and his friends to feast on and as punishment for the offence. It was a punishment the chiefs relished.

The chief responded by sending a message to Nzeki, through the assistant chief, to either send one of his sons to school or give a cow to the chief. Ironically, the assistant chief had sons Ndingi's age but he had not sent any to school. Many locals perceived school as a place to receive punishment and the more the reason they did not want to send their children to school. They preferred giving a cow to the chief instead.

As luck would have it, Nzeki sent Ndingi to school. He met the head teacher, Mr Benedict Mailu to whom he handed over his son. He also carried with him ten cents and gave it to Mr Mailu.

"Take this," he told him. "Whatever my son needs, buy it for him." Ten cents was a lot of money then.

There was no wearing of uniforms or shoes those days among school-going children. Boys and girls walked barefoot and wore whatever they could to school. His class had between fifteen and twenty pupils, all boys gleefully walking along the dusty floors and bearing the punishment that the hard ground occasioned on their feet. Ndingi wore his first pair of shoes ten years later when he finished school.

Despite the enthusiasm to learn, Ndingi was not lucky. After only a year, Myanyani school was closed. The low level of enrolment made it unviable to run and those who wanted to continue with their education had to look for an alternative.

Ndingi's passion for education, however, could not allow him to drop off at that early stage. He sought an alternative and proceeded to Kabaa Mission School. All his former schoolmates were not that lucky. They dropped off and went home to graze their parents' animals and wait to follow in the footsteps of the peasantry.

In those days, boys who did not attend school spent all their time looking after animals by the day and at night would engage in Kamba dances. The dances formed the village's small awakenings, some sort of transcendence that transported them from the inanity of their lives to some form of meaning and which enabled them live one day at a time.

Few girls ever attended school. In Ndingi's days only two girls from his village went to school. One was later married to a teacher while the other proceeded up to Standard Eight, after which she dropped off.

Looking back, Ndingi still wonders why his father chose to send him to school instead of paying the fine. Maybe he had a strong sense of the boy's destiny, maybe he was acting under some propulsion too difficult for him to understand. Much more than this, he wondered why even after Myanyani was closed, his father was still keen to see him pursue his education, something that he obviously never had for the other family members.

After relocating to Kabaa, Ndingi was to stay for one year before hitting the road again. Just as he was settling down in the new school and new ways of doing things, Kabaa Primary School was also shut down, another victim of low enrolment. But this too did not daunt him and he moved to Etikoni Primary School, ten kilometres from his home. If the pursuit for a place to study was daunting, the sheer act of making it everyday to a school, ten kilometres from home, was to prove bone-breaking. In those days, there was no readier means of transport than a ride on the back of a donkey, which still was rare. Donkeys were not your every kind of animal. Vehicles were so rare that in some places, people had never seen a vehicle. There were no roads then and the few tracks were impassable. If Ndingi had to continue going to school, he was to either commute or look for some form of accommodation somewhere near the school. Better still, he could drop out and wait for the time when schools nearer his home reopened, rejoin and hope that all would be well till the end.

But his help was to come from an unlikely quarter. For it was not only the pupils who had been affected by the closure of Kabaa, the teachers too had been affected. The headteacher, Mr Simeon Matheka, was one of those who moved to Etikoni with Ndingi and he proved to be of invaluable help. He organised with shopkeepers at Mbiuni Trading Centre, which was the nearest shopping centre to Etikoni, to provide the young boys with some accommodation. Mbiuni was a small dusty backwater with a handful of shops from which the villagers bought their provisions.

The pupils who could not commute daily to their homes had to be accommodated at the back of the shops which bore small rooms that the shopkeepers rarely used. Ndingi was one of them.

This was a particularly trying time. The Second World War

was in full gear and the construction of the Nairobi-Garissa road was going on to supply weaponry and facilitate communication to fight the Italians in Somalia. The British Government was afraid of Benito Mussolini, the Italian who was leading the National Fascist Party and whose frequent sabre-rattling rubbed the colonial officials the wrong way. Mussolini used to brag that he would have breakfast in Nairobi and supper in Mombasa meaning that he never saw any difficulty in overrunning the British colony. The Government's main concern then was how to keep the Italians at bay.

Food was very scarce then. The boys used to fetch firewood to cook, but what to cook was a question they grappled with almost every day. They would wander around the market hoping to pick up some leftovers but more often than not there were none.

Thankfully, the shopkeepers were kind people. Ndingi remembers four shopkeepers who were particularly helpful. They were Mr Daniel Munuve, Mr Simon Ndile, Mr Pius Katiku and a Mr Kilovia. They would give the boys ten cents with which they would buy some food. With tearful gratitude, they received the money and put it to good use hoping for the day they would not have to beg again.

"I don't know why they gave us the money," he recalls. "Perhaps they could see we were hungry and took pity on us."

The wife of one of the shopkeepers was particularly kind. She would cook more food than was needed and give it to the boys. But she never let the boys know that she was cooking for them. Rather, she would tell them that they were leftovers from the day's supper. It did not take long for Ndingi to wonder why there always were leftovers in that family and not any other home, at a time when famine had struck. The truth dawned on him much later. Years after he had become bishop, he influenced the employment of the shopkeeper's son at the Bata Shoe Company.

"It was all done in gratitude," he says. "We could not repay her."

Over the weekend Ndingi and his fellow pupils hit the road, walking the ten kilometres to rejoin their families. Weekends were their happiest times. But this happiness was short-lived as one half of Saturday was spent walking home and the better part of Sunday walking back to Mbiuni. So they only had half a day in which to compress all their joys and forget momentarily, their misery. Much later, Ndingi was to write in his diary, "I only ate a meal once a day at supper time. A plate of maize made my supper"

To get the maize, they had to queue. They used to call this *mwolyo*, which means queue. When people talked about getting *mwolyo*, they meant queueing for relief food, which was distributed only once a week.

The teachers were strict. It was mandatory for all Catholic students to attend Mass and a register of all those who attended was religiously kept. One day in 1945, during the school holidays, Ndingi and two other boys missed church deliberately. Having left home ostensibly for Mass, they wandered off to play instead. When they saw people returning from church, they joined them and went home pretending to have come from church. After the holidays, the register revealed the misdemeanor. The punishment was a back-breaker. They were to draw water from a river two miles away from the school and up a steep hill using *debes*. They never dared miss church again.

At the end of 1945, Ndingi sat for the Common Entrance Examination in Standard Four. Despite all the hardships he and another boy called Ngili had endured, they passed well and were admitted to Kabaa Mission School the following year. Kabaa, one of the most prestigious schools in the district, had been set up by the missionaries and those who were admitted there were looked at with envy and a touch of jealousy. Kabaa was named by the missionaries after a Kamba word meaning 'better'.

When the missionaries arrived in Kambaland, they wanted to put up a mission in Kangundo but the Africa Inland Church was already there and had set up base. The missionaries were encouraged to go further to a place called Kombe because it was 'better' there. When they got to Kombe they were advised to move further on because it was 'better' there. When they finally got some place to establish the mission they called it Kabaa, meaning 'the better place.'

Ndingi's biggest joy came not just from passing the examination but from the fact that being admitted to Kabaa meant he would no longer cook for himself or walk ten kilometres to school. All over the village the talk was: "Ndingi and Ngili are going to Kabaa." Unfortunately Ngili was to die only two years later of meningitis. Ndingi saw him on the morning he died and his only consolation was that he was baptised just before he passed away.

Ndingi was happy that his dream for an education was, by dribs and drabs, getting nearer to fruition. But it was after his admission to Kabaa that he started wondering how he had kept going for five years, walking for twenty kilometres every weekend to and from school and cooking for himself. He was to remember how he had kept hoping that the lorries that transported sand from the riverbeds of Nditha to trading centres would pass by and give him a lift. On some days, which were not many, he would find himself on the back of a lorry lying on wet sand and tearing with gratitude at the benevolence of the lorry driver.

At other times he would be lucky to spot the parish priest's vehicle and the priest would unfailingly give him a lift. At the time, however, this did not look like a hard life. He had been so accustomed to hardships that it started to appear like it was his ordained course of life to walk all the miles and sometimes be awakened by pangs of hunger in the middle of the night. His admission to Kabaa momentarily provided a better time. But there were days he would wake up with a start, in the middle of the night, afraid that it was all but a lofty dream.

Destiny, it is said, has an infallible sense of timing. On one cold morning, a priest by the name Fr Paul Wallace came for a retreat with the pupils. Kabaa was run by missionary priests and was, hence, very strongly oriented towards Christianity and in particular Roman Catholicism. The soul-searching retreat that Fr Wallace visited upon the young pupils of Kabaa left them with a clearer idea of God and Christianity. At the end of it came the eternal question that was to irrevocably change Ndingi's life.

"Who among you would like to become a priest?" Fr Wallace asked.

The pupils looked at one another as if waiting for a collective cue before they could make a decision. But Ndingi did not wait for that cue. He promptly raised up his hand but at the same time looking around the room; his was the only hand up.

From then onwards, there was no turning back. Ndingi left Kabaa and proceeded for his Standard Eight studies at Kilimambogo Seminary. He was required to learn Latin, which was then, and still is, the official language of the Catholic Church and one in which Mass was said. At first, he was so poor in Latin that he wondered if he would ever master it. The Fr Rector, N. McCauley, was not impressed with Ndingi's performance in Latin. At one time, he remarked on his paper, *"Hutumii akili ukifanya kazi*" (You are not using your brain while doing your work.)

All through his stay at the seminary, his family, specifically his brothers and sisters, was still opposed to his joining priesthood. In 1948 his brother, Muli, sent him a letter stating that he had never heard of or seen an African priest. He asked Ndingi why he thought he would make one. If he did not leave the seminary at once, he threatened, he would not pay fees for him again. The fee then was Sh 63 per year. Ndingi responded that if it was God's will that he be the first African priest, so be it. He sat pretty and went on with his education. So filled with disgust were his brothers and sisters that they were openly overheard saying that it would have been better if Ndingi had died at birth. In 1949 he joined Kilimambogo Teachers Training College to train as a P3 teacher. He would return to the seminary in 1951 to join Form One after his Standard Eight Examinations.

He was to sit for another examination in Form Two. The Form Two examinations were critical for they marked an important turning point in one's high school education. But, yet again, luck was not on Ndingi's side. Bishop J.J McCarthy who was in charge of Nairobi Diocese under which Machakos fell abolished Form Two examinations in mission schools. Ndingi and another pupil, Urbanus Kioko, who was also to become a bishop, were moved to Kibocho (Moshi) in Tanzania to join the seminary in 1953. They were to stay in Moshi for three years after which they were recalled back to Kenya. The whole of 1956 saw Ndingi teach at a junior seminary.

What was strange about all this was that while Ndingi's parents knew he was in school, they did not know what he was studying. Least of all, they did not know that he was studying to become a priest. In 1957, when Ndingi and Kioko were again sent to St Thomas Aquinas Senior Seminary-Morogoro in Tanzania to study theology for four years, his parents still had no clue. At that time it was not usual for blacks to join priesthood and people who were enlightened enough to know what disciplines pupils studied in school were few and far between. It was enough to assume that those in school were simply getting an education. What kind, was an issue too complex to delve into at that time.

# CHAPTER THREE

## *In the seminary*

In 1957, Ndingi and Kioko were the only two students in their class from Kenya at St Thomas Aquinas Senior Seminary, Morogoro – Tanzania. There was also John Njenga but he was their senior and was more enlightened. Having joined the senior seminary earlier, Njenga's proficiency in Latin was impressive. As a seminarian, one had to learn Latin and it was Njenga who made the lives of the two Kenyans easier by teaching them Latin.

Morogoro was, according to Ndingi, also a hardship area. Walking ten kilometres and starving at the back pent rooms of Mbiuni shops may have looked like the ultimate hell but to be confronted by hardship at a place one expected to be better off was a touch too treacherous for Ndingi.

St Thomas was a hot place usually enveloped by an impossible climate. The quality of food was poor and in some cases hardly edible. The seminarians mainly fed on a diet of maize and beans with a generous supplement of weevils. The priests found nothing bad or unusual about the weevils but the students cringed at the inevitability of feeding on them everyday. To make matters worse, the students were afraid to protest. They feared the white priests who were known for their ruthlessness when it came to enforcing discipline.

## In the seminary

There were many times, however, when Ndingi thought of speaking out against what he and the others saw as gross injustice on their culinary tastes. But he knew he did not have the authority to do so and besides, protesting would have invited the label of a rebel.

Luckily for him he was made prefect. This was the much needed platform to voice out the many complaints and articulate the general feelings of his fellow students. He embraced the opportunity and immediately approached the Fr rector with the intention of telling him the unpleasant truths about the seminary.

"The seminarians are not given enough food," he told him, "and even then, the quality of the food is poor." If the Fr rector was struck by the irony of the boys who were complaining about the state of the food and at the same time were concerned that the food they were calling poor was not enough, he did not show it. But he was, to the surprise of Ndingi, more amenable to students' demands and needs than the other white priests. So he listened in silence and got a firsthand account of the horrors that were afflicting the boys.

"The mosquitoes are vicious and we cannot sleep at night," Ndingi continued.

The priest stirred from his seat.

"Is that so?' he asked.

"Yes, father," Ndingi answered.

"Are you sure that this is happening?"

"That is the whole truth and nothing else but the truth," Ndingi responded.

"Bring the others along," he said, "I would like to hear from them."

Ndingi shepherded the rest of the boys to the rector's office.

They all replied in the affirmative to the questions he had asked Ndingi.

Then, in a move that shocked all, the rector opened a drawer.

"Here, these are the keys to the store," he told them, "go and see if you can get better food."

On top of that, he allowed the use of mosquito nets and the wearing of long trousers. From then onwards, the health of the boys improved immensely. But also to improve quite considerably was Ndingi's standing among the other students who saw him as their redeemer at least on matters concerning the running of the school. This was a far much better man than the one who had almost made him leave the seminary.

Most students supported Ndingi but others did not wholly trust the Kenyans. They accused them of belonging to a 'Mau Mau group,' a serious charge given the Mau Mau uprising was already underway in Kenya.

Returning home in 1960, Ndingi settled on the last route that would see him to his final destination of priesthood. His first task was to formally announce to his parents that he would be ordained as a priest. He prepared himself for the mission, setting aside the day when he would break the news. He knew the news would shock some and perhaps please none. No one, in the family, he suspected, had an inkling about what priesthood meant.

In keeping with the tradition then, when one had some important news to tell the parents, he or she prepared some beer, poured it into a calabash called *nzele* and passed it around among the old men gathered to hear what he had to say. Each tasted the beer. Then his uncle rose and addressed Ndingi's father, "Can you ask your son to tell us what the purpose of this beer we are now drinking is?"

## In the seminary

Ndingi's father tasted the beer once again and addressed his son, "Go ahead, my son."

"I want to become a priest," he said.

"A priest?" one of the men at the gathering asked, standing up as if he had been stung by a scorpion. "What does that mean?"

Ndingi explained what that meant, outlining the fact that he would spend the rest of his life in the service of the Lord and that he would live away from home. They listened in consternation. Then one man, who seemed to have an idea about the lives of priests, rose and said, "But priests don't marry. Does this mean that Mzee Nzeki will never see an offspring from you?"

This brought some deathly silence upon the circle. They stopped drinking and waited to hear from the young man what exactly he was talking about and, more importantly, what madness would have propelled him into the life he now was saying he would lead.

As Ndingi explained, a protest broke out from his sisters. They started grumbling that he had made the wrong decision, that he should not be allowed to become a priest, that he should live the kind of life each had come to know. To go off without naming a child after one's father or mother was considered to be some sort of failure. This was said loudly enough for Ndingi to hear.

But Ndingi's father brought an end to the protest.

"Shut up all of you," he told them, almost shouting. "This is my home and when you have your home you can tell your children what to do and what not to do." This brought the grumbling to an end. But Mzee Nzeki had a few questions regarding his son's new life.

"What if you do not succeed?" he now calmly asked.

"I will come home," Ndingi replied.

Upon this assurance, Mzee Nzeki sipped some beer, then sprayed it on his son's chest and said, "If you do not succeed, this is your home. Come back." This was all the blessing that Ndingi required to embark on his new journey.

However, Ndingi's sisters were still not done with their protests. The following day, they followed their mother to the shamba and gave her a lecture about the decision Ndingi had chosen.

"Ndingi has made a very stupid decision," they protested.

One of the sisters even suggested that the young man had been bewitched and proposed that a medicine-man be sought to exorcise the demons that were now coursing through his head. His brother thought that Ndingi was too young and stupid to make decisions of that magnitude.

In the wider village the prevailing view was that the young man had been deceived by the Europeans to join their strange religion. They saw the impending ordination as some kind of death, some loss, some theft of their son by some wily, conniving Europeans.

"One day," commented one old man, "this son of ours will come back..."

But old man Nzeki was unrelenting in his support for his son's chosen way of life. He supported him right to the day of the ordination, an occasion attended by even those who had been vociferously opposed to it.

In many ways Ndingi's father was more fond of him than his half-brother. Though he hardly complained about Ndingi, he had a host of complaints about his half-brother. He was particularly irked by his habit of losing a cow each time he went grazing. Where the animals disappeared to remained a puzzle.

# CHAPTER FOUR

## *The big day*

For any seminarian, priesthood is the final destination after a long vocational road. All aspire to it but this aspiration sometimes clouds their expectations of that new way of life and sometimes prevents them from appreciating what being a priest is all about.

When he was in Kilimambogo, Ndingi struggled with his journey to priesthood. He had a clear vision of what he wanted to be and probably what kind of priest he wanted to become but he still needed a great deal of help from whichever quarter he could get it. This was mainly because there had been no other black priests with whom he could share experiences about being a black priest in a country used to white missionaries. Just before the ordination Ndingi attended a retreat during which he read quite a number of books about the expectation of priesthood. There were two priests who also helped him realise his call. One was Fr Nuggent who was in charge of Kabaa Parish and the other was Fr Finbar O' Sullivan, the headteacher of Kabaa. He spent quite some time with the two, learning and drawing a great deal of strength from them. As a seminarian, they put him under their wings and provided the 'spiritual nourishment' he needed to embark on the priestly voyage.

The day of his ordination is one he probably will never forget. Few priests do, even those who later leave the ministry. It is the actualisation of their dreams, the distillation of all their hopes and for some, some sort of reincarnation. You prostrate yourself at the sanctuary a deacon and you rise up a priest. It is the most important day of their lives.

On that January, 1$^{st}$ of 1961, Ndingi rose up early and contemplated the journey he had purposed to embark on. This was the first occasion of its kind in his village. Everyone was talking about it. "A black priest?" they asked, "and one of our own?" they consoled themselves. The people were familiar with white priests. Their idea of God and heaven was buttressed by the image of whiteness. God was a white man, many thought that heaven was populated by white people. A black priest was a touch unimaginable. What probably awed them more was that this black priest, the first of his kind, was one they knew, one they had seen grow, one they could relate with and one who talked their language. "Would he be a real priest?" they asked loudly.

From every corner of the village, and indeed the entire Machakos, the talk that January morning of 1961 was of the impending ordination. The Nairobi Archbishop, J. J. McCarthy, was to come in person and this was a figure that many had not been privileged to see. Multitudes travelled from all over. Catholics and even non-Catholic women turned up wearing white scarves to witness the historic occasion. The village was aghast at the picture of whiteness, an image they associated with holiness and the number of people who came to witness it.

For Ndingi, it was much more than just an ordination. He knew in more than just a simple sense that he had come to the junction of a long road and that there would be no turning back. His mind fleeted to those days in the seminary, to his brushes with the rector, to the day when he nearly quit the seminary

## The big day

on account of the harsh life in St Thomas Aquinas Seminary, Morogoro. It seemed a long voyage. But here he was, the centre of attraction, his life unfolding anew like the blooming of a rose at dawn.

When the Archbishop McCarthy laid his hands on him to signify the apostolic succession, Ndingi's life assumed some electronic lightness of being.

"The Father anointed our Lord Jesus Christ through the power of the Holy Spirit," he heard the archbishop's word seep into his consciousness in a solemnity that imbued the whole sanctuary where the ceremony was being conducted with unforgettable grace. "May Jesus preserve you to sanctify the Christian people and to offer sacrifice to God," the archbishop continued.

There was a loud applause from the congregation. Some could understand what was going on but for many it was the first time they were witnessing such a spectacle. And when the archbishop said the prayer of consecration, the congregation waited with bated breath, some yearning for the end of the ceremony, others curious to see what would happen next. "Christ the Lord, a priest forever in the line of Melchizedeck offered...," the archbishop started. It was a long prayer marked only by the deathly silence from the crowd.

When the archbishop lifted up the gifts, Bread and Chalice, to be given to the newly ordained priest, the congregation struggled to have a glimpse of the glittering instruments of worship as the young priest tried to internalise the archbishop's words. "Accept from the holy people of God the gifts that we offer to him. Know what you are doing and imitate the mystery you celebrate. Model your life on the mystery of the Lord's cross."

These last words meant that from then henceforth the newly-ordained priest's life had changed. Ndingi received the chasuble and presented his hands to be anointed with holy oil. The crowd roared. Raphael Ndingi, the son of Nzeki was now a priest, one of the first black priests in the country, a priest forever in the line of Melchizedek of old.

## The order of Melchizedeck

When newly ordained priests take to the route of their vocation, they normally focus more on their destination, the need to act out their vocation and be good priests, perhaps become bishops, than the pitfalls of the journey. At an early age, Ndingi had realised that the journey to priesthood would not be like the one to the seminary. From the day he received the implements of his apostolic calling he knew that things had changed. He was no longer at that point on the road when he could turn away and start afresh. Like a ship in the high seas, he had to follow the trajectory of his course, through the tidal waves of his calling until that appointed day that he would dock to give an account of his life to his Maker. If he needed prayers to see him to priesthood, then he now needed more of them to keep him in priesthood.

In his days in the seminary, Nairobi was a place Ndingi passed through but never lingered long enough to understand or know. Now, as a young priest, he had been posted to the city. Though Nairobi was not as imposing and confusing as it is today, it still was a wonder to those who had never been there. The tendency, then as now, is for those who visit big cities for the first time to lock themselves up, soak in the wonderment of the magnificence of the city and take a few days before they can venture out and start sampling its complexities.

Ndingi was stationed at Our Lady of Visitation church in

## The big day

Makadara, Nairobi, as an assistant priest. Although he had a short hiatus as an assistant priest in Tala, Machakos in 1963, he did not familiarise himself with the city, the proximity of Tala to the city notwithstanding.

Nairobi, as indeed most parishes in the country, was still largely under the missionaries. The parish priest at Our Lady of Visitation was Fr Michael O'Connor. O'Connor was a God-fearing man who took the young priest under his wing as he went about his first days as a priest in a big city. Ndingi would fondly and respectfully refer to the priest as *mzee* (elder).

But even before he was posted to this parish, Ndingi still had a burning desire to further his education. He felt that he wanted to raise the bar in his educational achievements and complete his 'O' levels. He sought the advice of an expatriate priest on the matter.

"You are too old," the priest told him. Ndingi was at first astonished. He was about to concur with the priest before pride welled up in him and he resolved to pursue secondary school education in spite of the disheartening sentiments. He privately enrolled for Cambridge School Certificate and started his studies in 1962. Some priests who thought this was a waste of pastoral time did all they could to discourage the young priest. But others, notably Fr Jim Kavanagh, encouraged Ndingi to further his studies. It was Fr Kavanagh who suggested a six months leave of absence in 1964 to enable Ndingi sit his examinations. Ndingi was to graduate with a Second Division.

After his graduation, he did not stay long at Our Lady of Visitation. He was sent right to the heart of the city at St Peter Claver's Catholic Church. This particular parish was to test the young priest's sense of orientation. For many were the times he got lost in the big city and had to devise ways of getting back to the parish. To have proper coordinates to his territory, Ndingi identified a few landmarks, some of which are still there today. One of them was the Khoja Mosque and the other one was the minaret of the St Peter Claver's Catholic Church. Nairobi then did not have the kind of skyscrapers it now boasts of. Besides, Khoja Mosque was one of the most famous bus and *matatu* termini for those coming into the city from the countryside.

It may be nearly impossible for those who know Nairobi as it is today to conceptualise the kind of life in the city then. The roads were dusty stretches and one could easily see one end of the city from the other. Traffic was light and the means of transport priests used were noisy and sometimes smoky scooters. Administrators, veterinarians and priests were the most distinctive users of the scooter. Upon hearing the sound of a scooter the residents knew that Father so and so was passing by as priests were firmly associated with this sort of transport.

And so, Ndingi with his scooter navigated the dirt roads of the city. Fr Michael O'Connor, his superior, used a Volkswagen Beetle. A new one those days cost about seven thousand Kenya shillings. It was cheap to maintain but the initial cost was a tall order.

At St Peter Claver's Catholic Church, Ndingi was also in charge of a segment at the Voice of Kenya radio (now Kenya Broadcasting Corporation) called Catholic Hour. It involved going to the studio and preparing a programme on Catholic faith. So passionate was Ndingi about this job that at one time he clashed with *Mzee* for failing to conduct confessions and choosing to instead go to the studio and record the programme.

"You are supposed to have been hearing confessions," he remembers *Mzee* thundering at him. "I would like an explanation as to why this was not done."

Ndingi tried to explain that he had to go to the studio to

## The big day

record the programme but *Mzee* would hear none of it.

"The programme is not a priority," he responded, "your pastoral work is."

"But that was the only time the studio was free?" insisted Ndingi.

"Go and tell that to the archbishop," retorted Fr O'Connor.

Ndingi did not want to argue much with *Mzee*. He went straight to the archbishop who had placed him in charge of the radio programme and stated his case. The archbishop wrote a letter to Fr O'Connor who, upon reading it, put the matter to rest with a taciturnity that still surprises Ndingi to this day: "You may continue with the programme," he told him and the tiff ended there and then.

Unspoken by many then was the uneasy relationship between the white priests and the upcoming black priests. The country had just come out of colonial rule and though not openly acknowledged, there was some lingering suspicion between the natives and the whites. Although not pronounced, these suspicions were also there in the Church. The few native priests then made no references to any discord or signs of it even when some arguments and differences pointed to unresolved issues between these two sets of clergymen.

The argument between Ndingi and his superior may not have been firmly anchored on these differences, but it was a pointer to the strained relationship between the native priests and the white missionaries. In fact this uneasy liaison characterised much of the early lives of the native priests including Ndingi. Bishop John Njenga who went to school with Ndingi remembers the icy relationship between the local priests and the white priests mostly brought about by cultural differences. But this queasy relationship influenced the way the white priests dealt with the locals. As young boys, Njenga remembers that they would attend Mass at the Chapel along City Hall Way, now the Holy Family Minor Basilica but when receiving the Holy Communion the priest would skip them proceeding to serve the whites in the queue.

"We waited and waited patiently," he remembers. "We used to say, 'this was okay, provided they do not deny us Jesus (Holy Communion).' After the priests were done with the whites they would then serve the blacks. This was a common state of affairs for many young and old Christians in many parishes in the country.

Though in most cases the white priests were helpful, there were some who were unkind. When he was the bishop of Eldoret, Njenga remembers going round to St Peter Claver's Church where Ndingi had been stationed earlier. There was a priest called Father Joe Lynch.[1] Father Lynch was feared by all. He had a mordant tongue and on the face of it, was rather impolite. When Bishop Njenga arrived at the Church one February mid-morning, Fr Lynch looked at him and asked, "What have you come to do here all the way from Eldoret?" The fact that Njenga was a bishop and Lynch was just a priest did not appear to bother Lynch.

"I have come to visit," Njenga replied.

"You think this is where people come to eat after coming from the bush?" asked Lynch.

"I will have my lunch here," Njenga replied.

After eating, Njenga told the priest, "Is this the food you were bragging about? It doesn't even have enough salt."

The priest did not respond. But softening, he told, Njenga

---

[1] Fr Lynch was known for his mistreatment of black priests. Some excused him saying it was his nature and was not a racist. Others felt he followed the pattern of the time.

## The big day

"Come over and spend the night here instead of going back all the way to Eldoret."

"No, I can't spend the night here. Your house is dirty and your linen usually unwashed."

This sort of grandstanding sometimes helped the black clergy to iron out disturbing issues with their fellow priests. Hostility sometimes turned into comedy and the two were able to get along quite well. Archbishop Njenga remembers that even Maurice Cardinal Otunga at times fell prey to this mistreatment. One day, the late Cardinal arrived at St Peters, wearing a coat over his cassock as he was wont to. Fr Lynch looked at the Cardinal and blurted, "You are wearing a coat, you think this is winter?"

Ever so humble, Otunga never responded. He proceeded with the business that had taken him there.

In many ways this theatre played itself out unnoticed by the Christians whose hearts teemed with love and faith for and in the clergymen. Some black priests, nevertheless, could not stand it and ran away. Ndingi, however, as exemplified by the case between him and the harsh rector, sometimes stood his ground and at the end of it an understanding would be found.

Unlike many priests who went on much later to become bishops, Ndingi did not do intensive pastoral work in parishes. He especially never served as a parish priest. Apparently the archbishop of Nairobi, Bishop J. J. McCarthy had other ideas for him, further putting to test the relationship of the native priests and the white ones at a time when the Church was encouraging more and more locals to take up priesthood and probably take bigger positions within the Church hierarchy.

Unbeknown to Ndingi, McCarthy was preparing him to take over the education affairs of the Church. Education was particularly important to Archbishop McCarthy who presided over the expansive Nairobi Archdiocese and whose word then was law. He was like the Apostolic Nuncio, answering only to the Vatican. Nairobi Archdiocese then extended up to Zanzibar and was probably the biggest in East Africa. There were only four jurisdictions then, namely Nairobi, Nyeri, Kisumu and Meru.

McCarthy's policy was to develop Africans by affording educational opportunities to them and preparing as many young men as possible to join priesthood and take up the leadership of the Church in Kenya. Not only did he start seminaries and convents but he also gave his home in Nairobi situated around the present Moi Nairobi Girls to Catholic sisters to train African young women to become nuns. Perhaps driven by the foresight of the inevitable independence, he started a rigorous recruitment exercise. He established a junior seminary in Kiserian way before the country got independence. The seminary had to be established far from the city because Nairobi then was a reserve of the settlers and establishments meant for black people had to be located in the outskirts. After independence the seminary moved to Ruaraka and it is now the present Queen of Apostles Seminary. This obviously did not please the white priests who often wondered why there was a hurry to place the Church in the hands of the Africans.

# CHAPTER FIVE

## *A priest among white missionaries*

As one of the first African priests Ndingi had to navigate what to him was an alien and sometimes treacherous road. The Church then was predominantly under the Holy Ghost Missionaries (HGMs) who had arrived in Kenya in 1889. In fact Catholicism in Kenya could be attributed to a great extent to the HGMs. They expended prodigious resources both human and material to bring Catholicism to East Africa; they started seminaries and convents; they were instrumental in bringing medical facilities closer to the people and the training of local priests was a central agenda to their operations. But, starting in Zanzibar in early 1870, the HGMs found themselves encountering many hurdles towards this goal. Lack of books and language barriers presented insurmountable challenges towards the training of priests.

By the end of the 19th century, the HGMs had not succeeded in ordaining a single African priest. But they were not to give up. Egged on by the conviction that education was the handmaid of evangelisation, they continued building schools and convents. Today some of Kenya's greatest in the educational sector are schools started by the missionaries: Loreto Limuru, Mangu High School, Kabaa High School, Precious Blood

Riruta, St Mary's Yala, Bishop Gatimu Ngandu Girls, and St Mary's Nairobi to name but a few, are some of the lodestars bequeathed the country by the missionaries.

It is however worth noting that at around this time Kenya was a catchment area for evangelisers. There were the Protestants hoping to cash in on the spiritual fecundity of the land and there were the Catholics, mostly represented by the HGMs, the Consolata Fathers and the Mill Hill Fathers. The Catholic Missionary Movement was at its peak. Some people have variously described it as a Godsend. In his doctoral thesis, *The Evangelisation Cathecumenate and On-going Formation System of Members of the Catholic Church in Nairobi Archdiocese* (1999),[1] Peter Kiarie Njoroge described the 19th century Catholic Missionary Movement as "nothing more than a special divine initiative on behalf of the black people of Africa."

The Holy Ghost Congregation had found its way into Kenya from Zanzibar and Mombasa. Its membership was mainly French. The Consolata Institute came into the country in 1902. As Mr George Kamau Muhoho[2] who was among the early African priests observes in his doctoral dissertation, *The Church's Role in the Development of the Educational Policy in the Pluralistic Society in Kenya*, "The Consolata fathers did not intend to evangelise the larger Kenya. Their focus was to evangelise the Galla tribesmen in Ethiopia but due to some 'insurmountable political difficulties' the plan was postponed, thus allowing the Missionaries to penetrate into the Kikuyu province in Central and Northern Kenya." The membership of the institute was

---

[1] Kiarie's thesis addressed itself to the impact and consistency of the system of evangelization used to convert individuals to become members of the Roman Catholic Church in the Nairobi Archdiocese between 1899 and 1999.

[2] At the time of writing the thesis, Muhoho was a Catholic priest. He later left the ministry, became a politician and is now a public servant.

exclusively Italian and therefore was known as the Italian Mission in Kenya.

The Mill Hill Society, observes Muhoho, came to Kenya as a result of the religious wars in Buganda and the members of the British Society were sent to prove that Roman Catholicism was not just a religion of the French. They occupied the whole of the Western Kenya following the creation of a new Vicariate in 1894.

The Missionaries worked in their well carved out territories: the Consolatas in Central and Northern Kenya, the HGMs in the East and the Mill Hill in the West had to take up the challenge of spreading the faith through the locals. At first, they achieved little success in the way of ordination of priests but with time progress was made. Although it was the policy of the Church in Rome to indigenise the faith in Kenya, this line was slightly misunderstood by a few white who ruled the roost in Kenya. While some white priests were helpful to the younger priests and totally committed to the communities they had come to serve, there were a few who engaged in unnecessary rivalry especially with the emerging caucus of black clergy.

Some white missionaries were openly antagonistic to the locals, leading to some unsavoury turf wars that sometimes threatened to divide the nascent Church in Africa. Ndingi wistfully and with a touch of regret recalls how the newly ordained priests were mistreated and made to feel like second class priests. Some of them wondered if they would survive but, invariably, their faith proved stronger than their 'small' tribulations.

"Those of us who were appointed persevered because of tenacity," he recalls, "It was a difficult time for us."

Their situation became more difficult even after ordination. Some black priests were still made to feel like they were in the seminary, especially after being posted as assistant priests to missionary-dominated parishes. Some were denied the use of vehicles and had to walk long distances to do their pastoral duties. This was at a time when a diocese had a handful of parishes and hence the distance between one and the other was monstrously long.

One priest gave an account of how some of the early local priests were treated by those they expected to be their mentors. He recalled a case where one priest, who later become a senior clergyman, was made to sleep in the sacristy and denied the use of a vehicle in a remote parish in Western Kenya.

It was heartrending to hear and see the clergyman's tribulations. He was already several ranks high in the Church hierarchy but the white priests among whom he had been sent to serve did not seem to recognise this. They denied him basic amenities and he had to walk for long distances to minister to the people. On the first day he arrived in the diocese he was denied accommodation and flatly told to go back to where he had come from. He had been sent as an auxiliary bishop but the priests were apparently not ready for one.

"This was a normal thing then," the priest says, "hostility blew like a quiet, cool breeze."

But as Ndingi recalls, rarely did the black priests hit back. They accepted the reality then and made a bold determination to ride the wave. Besides, they argued, not all the white priests were bad. In fact, he says, the really bad ones were a minority.

"The settlers were here to stay," Ndingi says. "They wanted to secure everything and they were finding it difficult to accept that independence had come and that things would have to be different."

Admittedly, the missionaries had done a lot in the country.

## A priest among white missionaries

They had established seminaries and they had cultivated vocations among their followers in their countries of origins. These young men had come to the country to impart the faith they had so painstakingly nurtured in their countries to a people who were just in the genesis of evangelisation. They gave their all to serve among a people whom they could not call their own but to whom, their faith dictated, they had to preach the Gospel.

On the other hand, the locals were just beginning to embrace Catholicism and the black priests were coming from backgrounds which were deeply steeped in traditionalism. Their parents were not Christians but were later to convert into the faith their sons had now totally embraced. Were these then the people who were being prepared to push the missionaries away from what they had all along regarded as their safe havens? Did they understand the imperatives of the new faith they were now embracing? Were they ready to navigate the eddies and currents of evangelism? Some missionaries clearly thought that the locals were not up to this task.

The emerging black priests were also not having it very easy on the local scene. Their communities were just waking up to a new phenomenon: that of black priests. Many thought that priesthood belonged in the realms of the white community among whose white priests were revered and feared. This, in many ways, contributed to the ignorance of the locals about the priests' lives. They took it for a given that if you were white, you were a priest. In fact in the Gikuyu community, there was even a saying that *gutiri muthungu na mubea*[3] (There is no difference between a whiteman and a priest.) Their lives and all their peculiarities were taken as a matter of course. Thus, the locals never wondered or seemed interested to know if the white

---

[3] The saying underlined the fear and sometimes mistrust that the people had for the white folk.

priests were married. The locals accepted them the way they were chiefly because these priests never allowed a chink wide enough in their closeted lives for the locals to take a healthy glimpse.

The houses in which they lived were like mythical castles. The locals only pointed at them with the crook of their fingers but very few ever wandered into the alcoves of those domiciles. This served to deepen the myth of the white priest and the more he remained mythical, the more revered he was. The locals accepted this state of affairs and they never bothered to know much about the white priests other than the fact that they were good and that they were men of God.

Now, the young men currently getting ordained were the sons of their communities. The locals had seen them grow and they knew them. They looked like them and they were closer home to their idea of 'familiar human beings' rather than the mythical, mysterious white persons around their parishes. They expected these black priests to behave in a certain way, a way that was understandable and more familiar to them. But as Ndingi recalls, even the locals found the new crop of black priests strange. These people were educated but they were not married and they had no families. And as many villagers came to understand, with disbelief, these people would never marry. To some communities, this was a difficult thing to accept. It was unheard of that an African man of marriageable age could choose to live a life of celibacy while everyone else was aching to find themselves wives and bring forth children. Questions and more questions unreeled themselves.

With time, these communities gradually learned to accept that their sons had been given up to the Lord. The fear of the Lord was predominant over the tribal proclivities and it was not hard for the priests to gain acceptance and favour in the eyes of his own people, many questions on their peculiar lifestyle notwithstanding.

However, it was becoming a struggle to find a level ground in a white dominated clergy. Some priests viewed this friction as a simple misunderstanding arising from a clash of civilisations. But, others saw it as a dogged determination on the part of the foreigners to hold on to and protect their turf.

If the white Fathers thought they would protect a territory long thought to belong to them, they were indeed in for a shock. Black priests were being ordained at a steady rate. There was Father George Gathongo and Father Kimotho wa Njeri who had joined the lot. Then there was the first diocesan priest to be ordained in Nairobi in 1942: Father Paul Njoroge Senior.[4] Then came along Father John Njenga[5] who was later to become Archbishop of Eldoret and later Mombasa and who was the second diocesan priest to be ordained in 1957. Ndingi had joined these ranks, having being the first black priest in Machakos Diocese to be followed by Bishop Urbanus Kioko who died in March 2008. There was late Ceasar Gatimu, who became the Archbishop of Nyeri and there was the late Emilio Njeru of Meru.

Many more were to follow and this, much as the foreign priests wanted Catholicism to take root in the country, was a legitimate source of concern to the missionaries who were afraid of getting edged out of the centrefold: a place they felt safest.

But far from this, this perceived friction was perhaps a necessary step in the development of the Church in Kenya. It was to give way to greater harmony among these two classes of priests most of whom today co-exist almost seamlessly in a manner that would never have been thought possible in the

---
[4] Fr Njoroge Senior went to Rome, and died a few years after his ordination.
[5] Fr Njenga has since retired and is now the Archbishop Emeritus of Mombasa.

early days. Many are the black priests from Kenya who today work in parishes in Europe and America and many are the white missionaries who still work in the country and live with the black priests without regard to race or colour.

In spite of these early hiccups, Archbishop McCarthy was firm in his foresightedness. He continued with his programme of Africanising the Church and in 1965 he appointed Ndingi Education Secretary for the Catholics in the entire country. Ndingi was to take over from Fr John O'Meara, an Irish priest who had a long history at the helm of schools and education in the country.

This, however, touched a live wire. When Ndingi was first proposed as the first African Secretary General of Education in Machakos Diocese, ripples of unease rocked the Church. J. J, as Archbishop McCarthy was known, had embarked on a classic mission to *e'pater les bourgeois*. The Church, the white priests believed, was being railroaded into accepting things it was not yet ready for. It was generally accepted that eventually black priests would take over the religious destiny of their country but that time was, in the thinking of many, way too far off.

It was particularly ambitious for J.J to think that a black priest would ably replace a white, experienced priest as the education secretary. A letter was then written by the Education Secretary in Machakos, Fr Pat Boran, to the archbishop stating that Ndingi was not qualified for the post.

Fr Boran's letter gave a list of reasons as to why that all important seat could not be left to Ndingi and asked the archbishop to reconsider his decision. An African priest, the letter contended, could not handle educational matters:

> While I appreciate the appointment of an African priest as education secretary of Catholic Schools, Machakos district, I consider it not opportune.

## A priest among white missionaries

The letter enumerated the massive duties that the education secretary was supposed to carry out and the enormous responsibilities he was supposed to shoulder. Some of them included ordinary secretarial duties, accounting, cultivating good relations with fathers-in-charge and expanding education opportunities in the district:

> The amount of ordinary secretarial routine work, together with the rather involved accounting system, requiring a more or less trained person outweighs the laudable desire of appointing an African to the post.

Most fathers-in-charge of missions were, understandably, white missionaries and Fr Boran's claim that an African Education Secretary would be under pressure from them was, in a way, quite true, if not conspiratorial. Fr Boran suggested that an African could only act as the secretary's clerk awaiting such time that his appointment to the all too involving post became opportune:

> I seriously doubt the ability of an African priest to attempt such things, and he will inevitably be under much pressure from fathers-in-charge of missions.

Ndingi says he does not know how the Archbishop responded but his resolve to have him as the Education Secretary was as undented as the resolve of the Machakos Education Secretary to have his appointment blocked. Ndingi was, however, quite miffed at the remarks of the priest and especially by the conclusion that an African priest could only serve as a clerk to the Education Secretary.

"This conclusion is revealing and indicative of the *Mzungu* mentality towards Africans even those who were equally trained in priesthood," he was to write in his diary.

J. J. went on with the appointment and posted Ndingi to the education office in Nairobi to work under Fr Sean Grogan. Fr

Grogan was the harsh rector with whom Ndingi had clashed in his days at the seminary. History was to repeat itself at the office. Fr Grogan apparently continued with his old ways and treated Ndingi as if he was an anonymous figure in the office. He could not be allowed to use the office without being chaperoned and there was an air of mistrust around him. Ndingi was to later complain:

"Working at the education office was not easy. There was a colonial attitude among those I worked with. I resented this. No keys were given to me. I could only go to the office in the company of other priests and I had to leave when they did."

Unable to take this kind of treatment, Ndingi contrived a plan. One afternoon, he took the main office keys and made a copy. Fr Grogan never came to know of it though he treated Ndingi with suspicion. In October 11 1962, Ndingi decided enough was enough and penned a letter to the Archbishop:

> I am afraid to say that I am not pleased with the way things are. I fail, therefore, to see how I can take responsibility for the Nairobi schools under the present circumstances created by Fr Grogan.

Ndingi also asked, in the letter, for an appointment with the bishop to explain his sentiments. The response from the Archbishop was to transfer Ndingi to Tala in Machakos where he had come from. Ndingi was happy to be back in Machakos "among a people whose language and customs I knew well and understood," as he was to remark later.

However, he fully was not to stay in Tala for long for J.J. McCarthy implemented his plan to have Ndingi run the educational affairs of the Church. He appointed him the first African Education Secretary General at the Kenya Catholic Secretariat. He was sad to leave Tala but happy to take up his new appointment. "I left my soul in Tala," he later said. He felt a little inadequate to fit in the shoes of Fr John O'Meara, who, despite the demeaning attitude towards blacks, he still had much respect for and whom he was to replace. But Ndingi, nevertheless, picked up the gauntlet and started on the job.

He was put on a salary of six hundred shillings and given a fuel allowance of one thousand shillings every month, an amount he was supposed to account for judiciously. Coming as one of the perks for the job was a Ford Cortina, a worthy promotion from the perils of a scooter.

# CHAPTER SIX

## *Education and a handy ally*

In his brand new car, Ndingi traversed the length and breadth of the country overseeing education matters as the first black man to hold the job. Education at the ministry was still in the hands of colonialists and Africans were still lagging behind in this critical area. It would then have been rough going for a black Secretary-General to push through programmes in a white-dominated ministry. Besides, there seemed to be some quiet hostility from the government towards Catholics. It was safe to assume that the previous education secretaries succeeded mainly because those who ran the Ministry of Education and some key departments in the government were mainly whites. The priests then found it easier to relate with them in an agreeable manner. But Ndingi would find it rather tough in this new area. Luckily for him, he was to find a worthy partner in a young African man who was then the Assistant Director of Education at the ministry and who seemed to share his enthusiasm for education among the natives. His name was Moses Mudamba Mudavadi.[1]

As luck would have it, the government then was in the process of introducing the 'A' level system of education. There was hence notable expansion of schools in many parts of the country. But for some reason, most of the schools being established

---

[1] Mudavadi later became a key ally of Moi's and a fierce KANU loyalist. He was also to become Minister for Basic Education in the Moi era. He is the father of Wyclife Musalia Mudavadi.

## Education and a handy ally

then belonged to the missionaries of the Anglican church. The colonial government rarely granted Catholics leave to upgrade their schools. This reluctance had its genesis in some unspoken historical reasons.

The early Catholic missionaries were seen as latecomers and they were not, so to speak, easily identifiable with the cause of the colonialists. The Catholics were seen as indifferent to politics and did not want to be entangled with what was happening at the political front. In his book, *A Century of Catholic Endeavour, Holy Ghost and Consolata Missions in Kenya*, Fr Lawrence Njoroge suggests that while the Catholic's so called indifference to politics may have appeared to be so, it was not necessarily the case.

> On closer analysis, theirs was not a policy of indifference to politics nor an apolitical stance, but precisely one arising from a calculating perception of the complexity of the situation. The Spiritans, (HGMs) soon after their arrival in Kenya, saw the inherent dangers lurking behind too close an association between government and missions.

Exactly how 'complex' this situation was is borne out of the fact that the Holy Ghost Fathers, as Fr Njoroge observes, "were acutely aware that they were trying to gain a foothold in a territory controlled by the British..." They had to tread carefully. But this neither endeared them much to the colonial administration nor to the locals who saw all whites as belonging to that oppressive class against which one day they must rise.

The Catholics seemed to appreciate and agree that the politics of the day had become a gargantuan entelechy combining hundreds of pieces, both political and social and through which they had to navigate delicately.

Yet, far from politics, the Catholic agenda those years

concerned itself more with education than politics. This agenda stretched back to the late 1920s when it began to emerge that the Catholic evangelisers laid a special significance on education as the main tool for their work. Fr Njoroge notes that during a key conference of the Catholic Ordinaries held in Nairobi in November 1928, all the twenty-five resolutions save for two, dealt directly with educational matters. In fact, in 1927, Arthur Hinsley who was then the Rector of the English College in Rome, from 1917-30, was appointed by Pope Pius XI to promote Catholic education in British Africa.

As Fr Njoroge notes, Hinsley, as indeed Rome, believed, that Catholic growth would be achieved most effectively through education rather than by any other means.

Hinsley was against the cooperation of the Catholic clergy and the government in ensuring that educational matters were given priority in the Catholic agenda. He insisted that "for Catholic children, there should be Catholic schools with Catholic teachers and a Catholic atmosphere."

The appointment of Ndingi as the first African Secretary–General of Education in the Catholic Church in Kenya should then be seen as part of the then continuing policy of educational expansionism within the Church at the time and its recognition of the crucial role that education would play in evangelism.

But the colonial director then was quite harsh on the Catholics, Ndingi recalls. Yet it was him that they had to approach to seek approval for expansion of some schools. As Education Secretary, the seemingly herculean task of getting the schools approved fell to Ndingi. It was a task he had to perform if only to prove that the Archbishop had not made a mistake in appointing him Education Secretary. But the Colonial Secretary then, had placed a number of hurdles which the Church was finding difficult to surmount. It was easy to deduce why the colonial administration might have been a touch too hard on the Catholics when it came to educational matters. In the first place, the early Catholic missionaries had a different view of education from that held by the government. As Muhoho notes, they loathed to be controlled by the government since their mission was to evangelise through education. This was a view widely held and understood by the colonial administration and which they brandished, with the fury of a sacramental unction, at any one who cared to listen.

"It must (also) be remembered that many missionaries are not trained teachers and do not view education as of greatest value 'qua' education, but merely as a medium of transmission of Christian belief," Muhoho quotes the then Provincial Commissioner of Mombasa, a Mr Hobley, as remarking.

Muhoho observes that "Independence from government control, independence to preserve their 'rights as missionaries', independence to develop a system with Catholic religious character for Catholic schools, was the policy followed in those early years even to the sacrifice of losing [sic] government grants-in-aid."

Further, the missionaries wanted to educate the natives at 'their own speed', to let them acquire a smattering reading and writing without intellectualising them too much to the extent that they would lose interest in manual work which was needed of them at that time.

"I believe in education for the natives to a certain extent," a white priest, Fr John Bergman, is quoted as saying. "Writing and reading... I am not in favour of teaching English. It spoils the natives. It gives them a swollen head and they become a dishonour to you unless they are well grounded in religion.

Education does and makes natives swollen-headed."

This pursuit of independence left the Catholic Church isolated. In fact, they were hardly represented on the Native Schools Examination Board and the many other educational boards. They lacked government assistance and they found themselves in a crisis simply because they were not seen to cooperate with the colonial government.

The presence of Mudavadi then came as a handy relief to Ndingi. He waited for the colonial director to go on leave and presented the long list of the schools that the Catholic Archbishop wanted approved to Mudavadi. Arriving at the Assistant Education Secretary's office, one early morning in 1962, young Ndingi found Mudavadi in a jovial mood. He already seemed to know why Ndingi was there, for after just a short conversation Mudavadi asked him, "Which schools did you want approved?" Ndingi gave the names including those of one school in Nakuru and another in Giriama land in the Coast Province, and a host of others spanning the whole country.

"No problem at all here," Mudavadi said to the eternal gratitude of Ndingi. He reached for a pen across his desk as Ndingi watched nervously. At first, he thought he would cross out some names but he gleefully watched as Mudavadi meticulously appended his signature, cancelling none and approving all.

"Mudavadi was kind, understanding and almost fatherly," Ndingi recalls. "He would advise you on what to do and he would always listen."

What Mudavadi did shocked the colonial administration. But it could not be undone. In the absence of the colonial director, he had the authority to approve and disapprove and his ruling was binding. Ndingi expected the colonial administration to be hostile, but there was no open hostility shown following

## Education and a handy ally

Mudavadi's move. Or so, Ndingi thought. The real truth was to be known later when, accompanied by a nun, Ndingi went to see the Colonial Secretary in a bid to have Loreto School in Limuru approved. Naively expecting to be accorded the same treatment that Mudavadi had shown him, Ndingi and the nun announced themselves at the Education Office. The Colonial Secretary, perhaps remembering what had transpired in his absence not a long time back looked at the two and screwed up his lips as if the room had suddenly acquired foul air. He flatly refused to give the approval. Ndingi was taken aback. But more upset was the nun who had accompanied him. On their way out, the nun loudly banged the door behind her, startling the Colonial Secretary. This displeased Ndingi:

"You don't do that," he growled at the nun. "I need to come back here again. I need to press that case and I need this man." The nun did not apologise.

Not too long afterwards, he went back to implore the Colonial Secretary to approve Loreto School, Limuru. The Colonial Secretary would hear nothing of it. It took the intervention of Mudavadi to finally have it approved and the Church promptly went on to establish Loreto School and also upgraded other secondary schools to 'A' level streams. This greatly pleased the Archbishop. The man whom the white priests had thought could not handle educational matters was beginning to prove his mettle.

Mudavadi, one of the few educated men in Kenya then had a passion for education. He had been a teacher before and he had worked in the ministry long enough to know that there was money allocated for education. It baffled him a lot to know that the colonial administration was dragging its feet on the question of education for Africans as he really wanted Africans to be educated.

His contribution to the early expansion of Catholic schools in Kenya was to remain appreciated until his death on 20th February, 1989. Whenever Ndingi met him, he would remind him that the Church owed its expansion of schools to him and would greatly thank him for that.

The following two years saw a marked improvement in the education sector within the Church. In his Ford Cortina, Ndingi travelled far and wide and his association with education within the Church took a special angle.

# CHAPTER SEVEN

## *First black bishop of Machakos*

One early morning in 1966, the apostolic delegate of Rome, Archbishop J.J McCarthy called all African priests for a meeting. Part of the agenda was the administration of the Church in Kenya. The sees (Catholic Church administration boundaries) were becoming too big, yet the population of the African priests was still far too small compared to that of the Europeans.

"I want to divide the Archdiocese of Nairobi," he informed them. This meant creating more dioceses in the outlying areas like Machakos, Muranga and Ngong, but the African priests were not for the idea.

"Before you divide it," they told him, "equip us with more education to enable us handle the challenges that this would present."

McCarthy listened in silence as the priests extolled the need for them to be further educated. Most of them, including Ndingi, had only gone up to Fourth Form, acquiring only diplomas in philosophy and theology and felt that they were not adequately educated for the task ahead. McCarthy concurred and the process for further education, for some of the early African priests, was set in motion.

But before Ndingi could be sent away for further education, a replacement had to be sought for him at the education secretariat. The bishop looked for someone to replace him without much success. In a way, this gave Ndingi some joy at the seeming indispensability he had cultivated at the office but this joy was to deflate into disillusionment. The Bishop simply went for the next in line, Fr Nicodemus Kirima, and handed him the scholarship.

Ndingi, however, was not to wait for long. In 1967, Fr Isindore Onyango was selected to replace Ndingi at the education secretariat and off Ndingi went to study History and Political Science at St John Fischer College, Rochester, in the USA. He was to graduate with a Bachelor of Arts degree in History and Political Science. The college later awarded him an Honorary Doctorate in Law for his notable scholarship and courage in standing up for the rights of the underprivileged. And it was not just the rights of the underprivileged he stood up for, it was also his rights especially when he felt oppressed. This was illustrated by an incident during his stint at the college. Ndingi was a bright student but one day, however, he was awarded a D score in one of the subjects. This got him horrified as he knew he could not have scored a 'D' judging from his earlier performance. He objected to the mark and confronted the teacher. After a long argument, the teacher admitted that he had sought students' help to mark and that they were the ones that had given him a score of D. The mistake was corrected and the students were never to participate in marking again.

His short stint at the college was all the preparation he needed to enable him handle the challenges that his superiors had already set out for him. Back home, word was rife that the country would have its first black bishops soon. There was already a reasonable number of practising black priests and rumours were doing rounds that it was time for them to move

## First black bishop of Machakos

to the next ladder in the hierarchy of the Church.

Meanwhile, Archbishop McCarthy had already started holding meetings with Christians to gather their views about the subdivision of the Nairobi Archdiocese and the possibility of an African bishop. One meeting held on March 3, 1968 at Our Lady of Visitation Mission, Nairobi, discussed at length the division of the Archdiocese. Also discussed was the possibility of an African bishop taking the mantle of the newly created dioceses. Some, however, opposed the move citing shortage of priests.

Another meeting held on April 7, 1968, at the same venue heard different views. Most people, especially those from Kiambu and Nairobi opposed the subdivision of the Archdiocese again citing shortage of priests. But the delegates from Machakos[1] took a different view. They wanted the Archdiocese not only divided but they also wanted their own diocese headed by an African bishop.

Almost all, however, felt that it was time an African was appointed bishop and some names were floated. They included Msgr John Njenga, Fr Ndingi, Fr Kirima and Fr George Muhoho. These were some of the black priests who had been sent abroad and in whom the Christians back home had a lot of hope. In fact, Ndingi would get letters from the faithful back home when he was in school who updated him on what was happening in town. Some of the people were supremely confident that Ndingi would get the appointment and the only question, as far as they were concerned was, when.

It then came as no surprise to him when, one morning as he was going about his chores at the college, Ndingi received

---

[1] The Machakos people had already started agitating for one of their own to be appointed bishop in the diocese. Ndingi's name had been variously mentioned.

a letter appointing him Bishop of Machakos Diocese. Though he somehow expected the appointment, he did not expect to be appointed so soon, more so while he was still away.

He was to be, not only, the first black bishop of Machakos but also the first for the newly created diocese. This was during the reign of Pope Paul VI. It should be recalled that this was at a time when the Church had just emerged from the intensity of Vatican II summoned by Pope John XXIII and whose far reaching changes the Church was struggling to implement.

This period is also described by critics as one of the most trying periods in the history of the Church. After the death of Pope John XXIII, Giovanni Battista Montini, Archbishop of Milan, who was to become Pope Paul VI found himself holding a church in crisis. It is said that his predecessor Pope John XXIII had foreseen this and had a word for his successor: "Amleto" (Shakespeare's Hamlet, a tragic figure at a trying time).

"Under this wavering and unlucky Pope, the postconciliar church went off the rails. All over the world, but particularly in the Americas and Europe, discipline became shaky or even broke down. Thousands of priests gave up their vocations and married..."[1]

There was one big consolation for Ndingi. These problems were not being experienced at home where he was supposed to go back and minister. The Church in Kenya had its own challenges and it had little to do with the postconciliar crisis. Its main challenge was indigenising the clergy and building up the nascent diocese for the greater growth and good of the Church.

Having graduated from St John Fischer College, Ndingi felt ready to face these challenges. There was no crisis of faith back

---

[1] Paul Johnson *Kitchen Pope, Warrior Pope: Time Magazine* Dec 26 1994-Jan 2, 1995.

## First black bishop of Machakos

home and the one challenge Ndingi had to face head-on was the growth of the Church and especially the running of the diocese of Machakos. It was not even a decade after the country had got its independence and to some, it was still unthinkable that a black person could be in charge of a predominantly white clergy. In the case of Ndingi, as bishop of Machakos, he was to have under his charge the Holy Ghost Missionary priests who mainly predominated the see. How would he fare? How would he move the Church from where it was to a point where the local people would see it, not as a white man's church but also their church? All eyes would be on him for the next two years.

Thus, when he made his journey to Kampala on June 3, 1969 to receive the purple hat from Pope Paul VI, he did so as the first African bishop to be head of a diocese. However, he was not the only one from Kenya. There was Bishop Emilio Njeru who was also going to receive the purple hat the same day and twelve other priests, among them the controversial Zambian Archbishop Emmanuel Milingo, were to be consecrated bishops that day.

The occasion was also used to canonise the martyrs of Uganda with the climax of the occasion being the consecration of the twelve. This marked the beginning of Ndingi's long journey into episcopacy.

# CHAPTER EIGHT

## *Home in Machakos*

Machakos, a district in the Eastern part of the country, is about 70 kilometres from the city of Nairobi. The diocese of Machakos was carved out of the greater Nairobi Archdiocese then being administered by Archbishop J.J McCarthy.

Principally, because most of the Holy Ghost Missionaries were nestled in that part, the place was mainly controlled and administered by the HGMs who had done a sterling job of evangelising, building schools and churches and ensuring that the Catholic presence was highly felt there.

In spite of the missionary presence, Machakos was, so to speak, still a virgin territory where real growth of the Church and modernity were concerned. The people were used to the white Fathers and they believed that the Church belonged to the white Fathers. There was, hence, the challenge of making them feel that they were as much a part of the Church as the white Fathers and that faith knew no racial barriers.

One good thing though was that Ndingi was a native of Machakos. The day he was consecrated, the people of Machakos broke into song and dance, hailing the return of their son and the creation of their own diocese headed by one to whom they could relate and speak the same language. There were only six African priests in the entire diocese and when Mass was not being said in Latin, it was said in very broken Kamba. But to their delight, here was a priest who could speak their language fluently.

At his consecration, Ndingi told the congregation: "We promise to carry our responsibilities without fear or favour, following the Lord to the point of being crucified if need be. A Christian must live according to his faith. This demands sacrifices – great sacrifices, small sacrifices – day in, day out."

This stand may have passed as just mere rhetoric but it was to define a good part of Ndingi's episcopacy and to a larger extent, his personal life and the way he conducted his affairs.

Still, the challenge for the newly consecrated bishop was to create an atmosphere where the people could embrace the Church, feel a sense of ownership and belief that their sons and daughters could also serve the Church in the very capacities that the white people were serving; a situation where the people could identify with the Church. But to do this, Machakos had to get in the habit of churning out young men and women into seminaries and vocations. The first task for Ndingi then was to cultivate vocations to ensure that within a few years, the diocese would be appreciably in the hands of the natives.

Machakos then had only fifteen parishes. With only six African priests, most of whom were assistant priests, nearly all the parishes were in the hands of the Holy Ghost Missionaries. But within the first year, the diocese had sent five young men to St Thomas Aquinas Seminary. This number increased every year with the first ordination of a local being experienced eight years later, long after Ndingi had left the diocese.

There was also the problem of the upkeep of the seminarians. Though the missionaries helped a great deal, the local people had to learn to support their own sons and daughters. With this in mind Ndingi started raising funds from each parish every year in support of the seminarians. The first year, he managed to collect only three thousand Kenya shillings, the second year, ten thousand shillings and subsequently twenty thousands shillings. This collection still goes on up to this day with the amounts going into tens of millions of shillings per year.

These collections succeeded in part because the people of Machakos felt that by doing so they were not only supporting their dioceses but they were also helping one of their own to succeed.

"They strongly felt that they had to produce many more like Ndingi," observes a priest in the diocese.

One distinct feature of the new young bishop was his emphasis on the need for Africans to be respected in the Church. No longer would Africans be comfortable being regarded as natives, badly in need of evangelisation or civilization from the West but as a people to whom the Gospel had finally arrived and who had the capacity to promulgate and spread it. This was amply demonstrated by the fact that an African bishop was already head of a diocese and many more were waiting in the wings.

Understandably, this rubbed some of the missionaries the wrong way and some would view Ndingi with suspicion. The fact that he commanded a lot of following in the area meant that his position as the pastoral leader of the diocese had been monstrously validated. What this inevitably meant was that the authority of the missionaries was being eroded by this African priest to whom they now had to report.

As happens when the status quo is threatened, there was quiet resistance to Ndingi. He would have liked to believe that most of the missionaries were totally supportive of him but there was that unspoken feeling that the Church was not ready

## Home in Machakos

for a black bishop in an area that had been firmly in the hands of the missionaries.

As fate would have it, Ndingi was to leave Machakos after two years. There was an outcry over his removal from Machakos Diocese, which did not get another bishop immediately and was instead left in the hands of a Holy Ghost Missionary priest, Fr Edward Tieanan. As they say in church circles, *Roma locuta, causa finita* (Rome has spoken. The matter has ended). Ndingi had to leave. Fr Tieanan was to preside over the diocese for a year before Bishop Urbanus Kioko was appointed to take over.

Ndingi's departure from Machakos after such a short stint has remained a source of fertile speculation. Was it his clash with some missionaries that led to the precipitate departure? Was it his outspokenness especially against the excesses of the Kenyatta government?

Young as he was, Ndingi had started rising out of the mould of reticence to challenge the orthodoxies of the time. While the other Kenyan bishops then were unwilling to criticise the Kenyatta government, Ndingi took up the challenge and started speaking against social injustice then.

Around that time, there was some secret oathing being carried out by members of the Kikuyu community. This followed the tragic murder in 1969 of politician Tom Mboya which drove a wedge between the Kikuyus and Luos. Some Kikuyu leaders began organising secret oathing ceremonies meant to ensure that the presidency never left the House of Mumbi (the Kikuyu community)[1].

The Catholic Church's voice then was not strong in the denunciation of the oathings and the protestants rose up against it, culminating in the martyrdom of one of their pastors

---

[1] Njoroge Lawrence, *A Century of Catholic Endeavour.*

in Kiambu. In the muted reaction by the Catholic Church to this crisis, Ndingi rose up to voice his concerns. He publicly challenged the Kenyatta government to explain the oathings and why the Kikuyu were being asked to pay homage to Kenyatta in secret.

He declared that he, too, would like 'to go to the moon', a euphemism for the oathing ceremonies as buses and lorries ferried people to these secret rites at night.[2] This was also the year that the first person on earth had landed on the moon, hence the term 'going to the moon.'

The Kenyatta regime may have brushed aside Ndingi's opposition, but it could not do so for long. Realising that the oath-taking was bound to polarise the entire country, two other priests John Njenga, then the Vicar General of Nairobi Archdiocese, and Ceasar Gatimu of Nyeri raised the matter with J. J. McCarthy.

"Your Grace," Bishop Njenga, now retired, remembers telling McCarthy, "it is true that people are taking the oath. We need to confront Kenyatta about this."

J.J, ever a diplomat, listened and said, "You know Kenyatta is my friend. You are a Kikuyu like him. You and Gatimu should take it up with him, after all you are the Vicar General."

Since Ndingi had already voiced the Church's displeasure at the oath taking, Njenga toyed with the idea of including him in the delegation to see the President. But he later thought it would carry more weight if they went to see Kenyatta as Kikuyus and openly voiced the Church's displeasure at what was going on. Njenga sounded off Gatimu who was at first reluctant.

"Njenga," Gatimu told him, "it's not true what they are saying about the oath. I met Mathenge (Isaiah Mathenge was then a

---

[2] Ibid

## Home in Machakos

powerful provincial commissioner in the Kenyatta Government) and he assured me it was not so."

Gatimu was wavering, Njenga noticed. In many ways Gatimu lacked the courage to confront Kenyatta who was his friend. The mention of Mathenge was meant to show that top officials in the government were not privy to the oathing thus they did not consider it a matter serious enough to warrant a delegation to the President. Njenga at that particular point wished Ndingi had accompanied them. He missed Ndingi's courage.

"It does not matter who you met," Njenga insisted, "but the fact is that people are taking and giving oaths."

"If it's true, what do you want us to do?" Gatimu asked appearing malleable to Njenga's forthrightness on the matter.

"We must go and see Kenyatta," he said

Arriving at Kenyatta's home in Gatundu one morning, Njenga, Gatimu and Fr Joachim Gitonga who was then the Secretary-General of the Kenya Episcopal Conference, found Kenyatta and his feared and immensely powerful bodyguard Wanyoike wa Thungu waiting for them.

"How are you Gatimu?" Kenyatta greeted them "Why have you come to see me with all these *wazees*, is the country burning? "We have come to visit, *Mzee*," Gatimu said.

"You are the pith of the nation," Kenyatta told them, "but because it is you who have come, then tell me what has brought you here." All of a sudden, Kenyatta grew serious. At that juncture Gatimu read a letter in which the Church was asking the government to stop the oathing. When he finished reading the letter, Kenyatta took the phone and called Charles Njonjo, the then powerful Attorney General in his government.

"I have some visitors here led by Gatimu. Come and hear what they want."

Njonjo, a staunch Anglican, asked if there was an Anglican bishop present.

"Is Obadiah Kariuki there?" he asked. Obadiah was the enigmatic Anglican Church Bishop. Kenyatta said no and Njonjo did not turn up. Njonjo was and is implacably Anglican.

Afterwards Kenyatta, aware that what Ndingi had started was now reaching a crescendo with the visitation of the three clergymen, proceeded to give them a lecture. "When we were students," he started, "we were told that the Catholics had their bell, the Anglicans likewise and no one would ask the other anything since each had freedom of worship. If this was how things were, why would you interfere with the Agikuyu people when they sound their bell?" He posed and looked at the three gentlemen in the eye.

"Gatimu, Njenga, people in my constituency are Catholics, yet they have all taken the oath." Then he posed and said again, "Gatimu, yes, people have taken the oath. They have really taken it."

The three were surprised at this admission. Then Kenyatta continued, "They have taken it but they have not denied their religion."

"Taking it, Your Excellency," Njenga intervened, "is to deny religion. Even Luos have a right to be respected."[3]

Kenyatta stared at the three. At this point, Njenga reminded the President that the oath business had also led impressionable people into forcing nuns to also take the oath. Kenyatta fixed his gaze on Njenga for a full minute then struck his walking stick on the table almost violently. It was his way of summoning Wanyoike.

---

[3] The mention of Luos is made in reference to the fact that at the time of the oathing there was bad political blood between Kenyatta and Jaramogi Odinga following the assassination of Tom Mboya.

"Wanyoike," he told him, "If I hear again that you have entered the nuns' houses, you will live to regret it." In fact, the words Kenyatta used in Kikuyu were, *"ukagera magenda mbia"* translated literally means you will pass where the rats passed when they were fleeing. And he dismissed the delegation.

The gesture from the three clergymen was hailed by all. But it was not lost on Njenga that Ndingi's voice had given the Church the impetus to confront the issue head-on and force the government to put an end to it.

It was not just in Kikuyuland that the oathing was taking place. In the Eastern Province areas of Yatta and Kangundo, the same scenario was enacting itself and still Ndingi was quite vocal about it. Mr Paul Ngei, one of the most powerful politicians during the Kenyatta regime, at one meeting between Ndingi and Kenyatta, attacked the bishop for his "allegations" that there was oathing in Kambaland. This was meant to cast doubts on the bishop's loyalty and credibility in the presence of Kenyatta. Later, Kenyatta called George Muhoho[4] aside after the meeting and told him in Kikuyu, *"Kamau, wiire muthikabu ndagetigire"* (Kamau, tell the bishop not to be afraid). Unbeknown to many, this first brush with the government was merely a shot across the bows. Ndingi was to distinguish himself as an acerbic critic of the government and of all that was perceived to constitute social injustice. The oathing issue was so important to him that he was not satisfied with the stance taken by his superiors with regard to it. He was to write in his diary:

> In connection with the oathing in Kenya, the Catholic bishops were not one. Many of them did not know exactly what was happening or if they knew, were afraid to speak out. The laity were worried.

---

[4] At that time Muhoho was still a priest and very close to Kenyatta, being his brother-in-law.

The Church did issue a pastoral letter on the matter. But it was not a strong letter. One bishop described it as a "Christmas peace message." Ndingi disagreed with the letter and issued one for his people, condemning in clear terms unchristian acts like oathing.

What surprised many was the fact that the young bishop knew no fear when it came to speaking out. While he respected authority, he seemingly feared no one. He had had a brush with the powerful Apostolic Pro-nuncio in Nairobi, Archbishop Perluigi Sartorelli, over issues to do with the Church's stance on some of the factors affecting the Church and the country then.

# CHAPTER NINE

## *Into a political hotbed*

As Fr Njoroge reports, it was after this brush with the powerful apostolist that the Pro-nuncio had him "translated" or transferred from Machakos to the Catholic Diocese of Nakuru. The transfer sparked off immediate and open protests in Machakos and dominated the pages in newspapers and religious magazines. Women faithful were particularly vociferous in their opposition to the transfer. The main problem being that Machakos would be left without a bishop. If Archbishop Sartorelli thought the people of Machakos would take the transfer lying down, he was wrong. He had to contend with rising voices of discontent.

When a bishop is transferred from one diocese to another, he continues to function as diocesan administrator. He may continue to fulfill the responsibilities of a bishop while taking care not to introduce any innovation or to prejudice any aspect of the governance of the diocese for his successor. He can also choose to decline the transfer after which the Church would be left to figure out what to do with the matter. Ndingi, however, graciously accepted the transfer. Apparently, he must have been under the impression that a Kamba priest would be immediately appointed bishop; a view that the people in the diocese seemingly held. But when Fr James Kavanagh, CSSP, was appointed Apostolic Administrator of the diocese, the people of Machakos felt like orphans. A great sense of injustice pervaded the air, a reality that vaguely demonstrated itself in the fact that Ndingi scarcely got any send-off from Machakos. The noise and controversy was to rumble on until Rev Urbanus Kioko was appointed the new bishop for Machakos on July 9th 1973.

"It was one of the most lively and breath-taking battles to watch on Kenya's ecclesiastical field," observes Njoroge, "Ndingi Mwana 'a Nzeki, ever so faithful to his promise of obedience, of course, accepted his transfer to Nakuru." But Ndingi had many admirers even among the Holy Ghost Missionaries. Fr Nil McCauley, Ndingi's former rector, wrote a letter of distress to Ndingi:

> I am writing to express my great regret at your transfer to Nakuru and personally your leaving us so. Your departure will be a great blow to the Akamba people of Machakos and the progress of the Church there.

Fr McCauley implied that the Church had not treated the bishop and the people of Machakos well and insinuated some foul play in the transfer:

> I'm appalled that such actions can take place in this age of Vatican II. I can still hold onto my love of and belief in the Church, despite the machinations and hypocrisy of individuals in the Church both in Kenya and Rome. Thank God they are not the real Church of Christ.

Fr McCauley appeared quite affected by Ndingi's transfer, lashing out at those he called hypocrites in Kenya and in Rome.

The people of Machakos also protested at the transfer, writing a strongly-worded letter to the nuncio and asking for a revocation. Another Holy Ghost Missionary priest who was also

## Into a political hotbed

a journalist, Fr Frank Comerford,[1] would openly question the transfer, thus lengthening the drama of the bishop's departure from Machakos.

Fr Comerford's was a direct challenge to Fr Sartorelli who was widely seen as the man behind the bishop's transfer. Sartorelli complained that Comerford 'was disrespectful to the person of the Holy Father's representative, especially in respect of the Ndingi affair.' The delegate demanded an apology, which Comerford gave. But as Njoroge notes, *The Catholic Mirror* was flooded with letters demanding to know why the priest had apologised. To many, Ndingi should not have gone and Comerford was right to point that out.

But as even those within the Church would tell you, no one dares the oldest religious institution in the world and comes out unscathed. *The Catholic Mirror*, joining hands with people like Ndingi was to become an acrid voice, which, on the face of it was capable of upsetting the seeming serenity in the Church. Pressure was brought to bear on Maurice Cardinal Otunga in whose diocese the monthly was being published and on Fr Comerford's superior, Fr Noel Delaney. By design or otherwise, Comerford went on leave and on coming back, *The Catholic Mirror* was almost defunct and Ndingi was off to Nakuru to start the new year, 1972, in a new diocese.

However, as Ndingi went on to take up the mantle in Nakuru, *The Catholic Mirror* changed its tune and sought to portray Ndingi's transfer as historic: "Bishop Ndingi has made history," it read on its front page editorial of March 1972. "In the course of two years he has been appointed the first bishop of two new dioceses, Machakos first, then Nakuru. His exit-

---

[1] Comerford was the editor of the *Catholic Mirror*, a highly respected daily written in both English and Swahili.

entrance has been bitter-sweet, a deep sense of regret and distress in Ukambani balanced by an almost audible sigh of relief and joy in the Rift Valley." *The Catholic Mirror* paid tribute to Ndingi in glowing terms calling him "the most unassuming and self-effacing of bishops."

"Total strangers are impressed by the Ndingi charm, the open friendliness, the readiness to listen, to laugh...and those nearer know how intrepid is the spirit behind that light-hearted gaiety."

If the Vatican thought they had heard the last of Ndingi, they had clearly misread the nature and character of the man they were dealing with, or, as the editor of *the Mirror* put it, the intrepidity of the man's spirit. A firebrand was in full plume here.

## No holds-barred in Nakuru

If Machakos was where Ndingi cut his teeth as a crusader of human rights, it was in Nakuru that he would go full monty in this regard. The people of Nakuru welcomed their first black priest and bishop on the early morning of January 30th 1972 with joy and fanfare. An estimated 20,000 people packed the Afraha stadium in a ceremony that started with a procession of bishops and clergy who included both Catholic and Anglican bishops, among whom was the Anglican bishop of Nakuru, Bishop Langford Smith. Ndingi was to cultivate a very strong relationship with Bishop Langford later.

In his first address to the people of Nakuru, Ndingi left no doubt as to what kind of shepherd he wanted to be. "I have come to work, not so much for you as with you," he declared. "I pledge myself to work with everybody, the government, the other Christian communities and other religions. I will give my heart and soul to my work, along with Pope Paul and my brother bishops, taking for my example the life of Jesus Christ who worked untiringly for all people; both rich and poor. In doing this I shall be doing what Christ wants me to do for the people of God. I stress that I will do so without fear or favour."

The last part of his pledge might have escaped some people, but throughout his stay in Nakuru the phrase "without fear or favour" was to become the defining matrix of the bishop.

Ndingi then invited the faithful to approach him whenever they needed him. "My house is your house, the door is always open. Anyone who needs me or wants to speak to me should come without fear. And when you come, do not call me My Lord. Call me Bishop, *Askofu* or Father. This is what I prefer."

Ndingi's coming to Nakuru was special in some way much as it was a loss to Machakos. In the first place it was not expected that a black bishop would be posted to the new diocese. In fact, as Fr Dennis Newman, the man from whom Ndingi took over in Nakuru (he was the administrator) was to record later, no other name had been floated for Nakuru[2].

The area had had a long association with the Mill Hill Missionaries and the Kiltegan. The latter had 28 priests, the former seven and there were only two Africans and one Goan. The name that kept coming up, was that of Bishop Willigers, MHM from Jinja. However, there was a remote possibility that Willigers could take over as amplified by the fact that Willger had been nominated in July 1967 as Bishop-Elect of the new Diocese of Jinja during the reign of Milton Obote in Uganda and there had been intense opposition then to a European being appointed bishop. There was thus doubt if Williger's appointment would hold. Some within the Mill Hill society suggested that he probably could be transferred to the new

---

[2] Father Dennis Newman, *One Hundred Years A-growing*.

Nakuru Diocese particularly because he had worked as priest in Nandi before his transfer to Jinja. But the Church was all too aware of what had happened in Uganda when Bishop Willigers was consecrated bishop instead of a Ugandan. The hostility of the Obote government, against the Church, that ensued led to an exodus of many missionaries with most spilling over into Kenya.

The Church too wanted to Kenyanise the hierarchy in the country which had been set up in 1953. This meant that bishops were no longer vicars of the Pope but bishops of their own dioceses and it also meant that missionary societies had yielded to the diocesan bishops the responsibility of evangelising their dioceses. In fact, in 1969, the Congregation for the Evangelisation of Peoples, also known then as *Propaganda Fide*, issued instructions regulating the relations between diocesan bishops and missionary societies and charting a new path in the way dioceses operated.

When Ndingi was then posted to Nakuru, it took the priests by surprise but it greatly enthralled the Christians there. *Ndingi who?* some asked. They could not figure out what Mwana 'a Nzeki meant and some found it a bit awkward pronouncing it. They would have preferred what they said was a "more Christian" name like John or Raphael. While the Kambas in Machakos had no problem with the name sounding as it did, the predominantly Kalenjin community took time to embrace it although they later became comfortable when they realised that it was their equivalent of "*arap* so and so" or that it simply meant "son of."

It was, as Fr Newman observed, an awkward name but at his insistence, it came to be adopted by everyone including the press and even Rome. But perhaps unbeknown to many, the choice

## Into a political hotbed

of name spoke volumes about the man's character and his very strong links to African traditions.

Ndingi was to experience his first challenge sooner than later. The Bull of Erection of the diocese had described the diocese as "Diocese of Nakuru" but this presented a problem. The Anglican Church and Church of the Province of Kenya, had arrived in Nakuru before the Catholics and had named their diocese "Diocese of Nakuru." This presented a clash of names. Ndingi had to make a quick decision to avert a full blown confrontation. He swiftly changed the name to Catholic Diocese of Nakuru (CDN) and then proceeded to cultivate good relations with the Austrian CPK bishop at the time, Bishop Langford-Smith and with successive Kenyan CPK bishops in Nakuru and other religious leaders including Muslims.

On his arrival in the diocese, Ndingi was presented with a new Volkswagen. It was out of choice, a choice he had made before arriving in Nakuru. He chose a Volkswagen because of its reputation for keeping out the dust in a really dusty place. After some time, however, he found the model unsatisfactory and he switched to a Peugeot. He was to drive this model throughout his two and a half decades of stay in Nakuru.

He also had his own ideas on where to live and work. The Apostolic Administration lived in a home at Lanet which Ndingi found unsuitable. He wanted to have diocesan offices in the municipality where he would work and live, as he believed this would accord him greater access to the people. The diocese had just acquired a plot in a plush area of Milimani which was not very far from town. He thought this would be suitable for him. The residence and diocesan offices were built on the plot and were ready for occupation by September 1972. However, Ndingi decided he should live in another new house to be built beside the Holy Rosary Church. He wanted to live among the people he would serve and found the idea of living in one place and working in another unacceptable. But the house could not be built in time for occupation.

Almost three months after he was installed the bishop of Nakuru, Ndingi's mother passed away on March 27, 1972. She had had a long battle with stomach cancer and Ndingi would visit her often. Her death greatly affected him but as he was to write later, it was a consolation that she had passed on after receiving all the sacraments of the Church. "I was presiding over a church function in Nakuru when I heard that my mother was very sick and travelled immediately after the function, but it was too late. My mother died before I arrived." Bishop Ndingi wrote in his dairy. "I cried for the death of my dear mother but I was very strong in faith." Ndingi himself had seen her two weeks before she died and blessed her. He was to lose his father four years later, on March 6, 1976.

At the time Ndingi went to Nakuru as bishop, the diocese comprised three districts: Nakuru, Kericho and Baringo, all covering an area of 22,942 sq. kilometres. The population of the area in the late 70s and 80s was nearly two million with Kericho District accounting for 836,000; Baringo, 270,000 and Nakuru 794,000.

Unlike Machakos which is mainly dry, Nakuru boasts of a volcanic landscape of lakes, residual cones and minor escarpments. The scenery varies from highland forest, to hilly pastures to fertile lowlands of the Great Rift Valley which are green for half the year and dry for the other half. There is also a large tract of semi-desert to the north where herds of camels and goats represent the wealth of the nomadic inhabitants.

Nakuru was then undergoing an influx of new settlers who

## Into a political hotbed

bought the land formerly occupied by the Europeans and who were slowly changing the demographic features of the place. Mainly occupied by the Kalenjin tribe, Nakuru was becoming a harbour for nearly all ethnic groups. At the time Ndingi went there, more than half the population was steeped in traditional religion, though many people still bore Christian names.

The diocese was originally part of the Uganda Protectorate and belonged to the ecclesiastical territory known as the Vicariate of the Upper Nile, the Prefecture Apostolic of Kavirondo, the Vicariate of Kisumu and the Diocese of Eldoret. The Mill Hill missionaries arrived in what is now Western Kenya in 1904 where the Church grew rapidly among the Luo, Luhyia and Kisii peoples. But Nakuru was occupied by white settlers and migrant labourers and by the Kalenjin people in the Kipsigis and Tugen reserves.

The oldest document in the present archives of the diocese was and still is a title deed for the Naivasha Catholic Church plot granted on 1st June, 1910. It was not until 1928 when the first mission was opened at Nakuru with Kericho following suit in 1935. However, both primarily catered for European and Goan Catholics and their migrant employees. Because of this, evangelisation of the blacks in the settled areas was greatly hindered. In the reserves, it was virtually impossible to penetrate the conservative attitude of the Kalenjin people. Things were made more difficult by the organised resistance from other Christian missionaries.

In 1952, a new missionary society called the St Patrick's Missionary Society or the Kiltegan came to the area and was given responsibility for Nakuru and Baringo district and the present diocese of Eldoret which was finally erected in 1968 and placed under the apostolic administration of the Very Rev

Dennis Newman, the man from whom Ndingi took over.

Nakuru was strange to Ndingi for various reasons. First, this was the second posting he was taking up as bishop in less than three years. He did not know the place nor the people of the area well. Secondly, he was the only black priest as the diocese was mainly in the hands of St Patrick's Missionary Society and Mary Hill Fathers. Bomet and Kericho were under the Mary Hill fathers. Nakuru itself had 10-15 priests, all missionaries. The first local priest to be ordained was Fr Peter Kairo, now the Archbishop of Nyeri. Even as Ndingi took over he was surrounded by white priests. A look at the structure then reveals how long it would take to effectively place most of the dioceses in the hands of the locals:

> The Vicar General: Very Rev Peter Coyle
> **Diocesan Consultors:**
> Rev Fr Anthony Prunty S.P.S
> Rev Fr Josef Gasser M.H.M
> Rev Fr John Jones S.P.S
> Rev Fr Romeo di Berti
> Rev Fr Thomas Kiggins
> Rev Fr Jeremiah Buckley
> Rev Fr Maurice Lwanga
> Rev Fr Peter Mbuchi.

It was among these people and the larger laity that Ndingi was sent to work. Immediately he was appointed bishop, he sent all the priests a letter dated December 31, 1971 reproduced here:

> To all Fathers/Nakuru Diocese,
>
> This is to inform you that I have taken possession of the diocese this afternoon and look forward to close co-operation with you all in the work of God.

## Into a political hotbed

I confirm you all in your appointments, and in addition to the faculties that you already possess, I give to each Father-in-charge the faculty of dispensing from the impediments of Mixed religion and Disparity of Cult on the usual conditions for his own mission. Copies of dispensations given should be sent or brought quarterly to me for record purposes.

I confirm Very Rev Fr Brian Cunningham as V.G (Vicar General) for the present and I have asked the existing consultors to continue to serve for the present. I have also appointed Rev. J.P Bohn to act as Diocesan Procurator, in charge of finances, for the time being.

As I am greatly in need of rest, I will absent myself from the diocese for a few weeks, returning a few days before my installation on January 30, 1972.

In the meantime, my blessing on the good work which you are doing. I look forward to meeting you all individually later. *Heri kwa Mwaka mpya.*

I remain,

Yours sincerely,

[+Raphael S. Ndingi Mwana 'a Nzeki]

Bishop of Catholic Diocese of Nakuru

This was his first stamp of authority in the new diocese where his work was largely cut out for him. The immediate concern here was the expansion of schools and in places like Baringo, the expansion of healthcare which in most places was either non-existent or in a miserable state. The district was dry and poor and its people needed immediate help. Ndingi introduced the Medical Missionaries of Mary and Sisters of St Joseph to tackle this problem.

Having been education secretary, education was never far from Ndingi's mind and buoyed by the Beecher Report of 1949 which advocated the immediate expansion of primary education, the Catholic missionaries had seized an opportunity for a breakthrough in this area. The report was a culmination of a government-sponsored study into the problems regarding the scope, content and methods of African education, together with its administration and finance. The committee concluded that there was evidence of a breakdown in "moral standards in African Society in recent years" and that to counteract this, it was necessary that greater emphasis be given to Christian religious teaching and moral instructions.

Its first recommendation was: "That the government continues to work with and through those voluntary agencies which have the teaching of Christian principles as part of their intention and that facility for Christian instruction be provided in all schools ."[3]

It also recommended that "the Christian Churches and Missionary Societies be encouraged to take a full share in the training of teachers and be afforded the necessary grants-in-aid to enable them to do so."

With these recommendations, Ndingi, working with the missionaries, set out to expand the educational capacity of the Nakuru Diocese. The Kenyatta government which proceeded to implement the report needed the assistance of the Catholic missionaries especially in the management of schools.

In Nakuru, schools under the Catholic management grew in numbers with a corresponding increase in catechumens. Under Ndingi, a Director of Catechetics (religious teaching) was appointed in 1981. Advised by a diocesan committee, the director was charged with organising among other things retreats and seminars for catechists and retreats for primary and

---

[3] Muhoho George, *The Church's Role in Development of the Educational Policy in the Pluralistic Society in Kenya*.

secondary schools. Between 1976 and 1980, 2,083 teachers, 40 per cent of whom were Protestants who taught the Common Syllabus approved by the Kenya Episcopal Conference were inserviced. The diocese also embraced the Religious Education Awareness Programme (REAP) which had earlier been started in the diocese of Kisii in 1979 and which was intended to increase religious awareness and to help Christians witness among parents, teachers and youth.

Under Ndingi, the Young Christian Students Organisation became a strong apostolate in secondary schools and today, it is found in almost every secondary school within the diocese.

The leaps being made in the growth of education in Nakuru were, of course, unprecedented. Ndingi became a father figure in the development of the larger Nakuru and in many places, he was not seen as merely a Catholic prelate but as a leader, some sort of governor at the helm of the area's developmental matters.

Diocesan priests were sent out for further studies in the first ten years to prepare them to take over the affairs of the diocese. Fr Francis Gichia was sent to Rome to study Moral Theology, Fr Wilhelm arap Sambu to the same place to study liturgy, Fr Joseph Gatamu to Catholic High Institute for Eastern Africa (CHIEA) to do Theology, Fr Cornelius K. arap Korir (Bishop of Eldoret) to Ireland to study Theology and Fr Patrick Kanja (Chaplain of the University of Nairobi) to study Sociology in the USA.

More and more young men joined religious congregations but more numerous than vocations to priesthood were vocations to sisterhood. The latter increased tremendously under Ndingi's reign.

Within the clergy there was social improvement too. Due

to the diverse nature of the place, transport had for long been a big problem. And because visits to the Mass centres and basic Christian communities were the main thrusts of a priest's work, the diocese established the principle in 1981 that every priest would have a car for his own use. In some areas of the diocese a four-wheel drive vehicle was essential. The vehicles were owned by the diocese with the logbooks firmly in the custody of the diocesan office.

Though some parishes in the more developed areas were becoming financially independent and could afford the running costs of the cars, most however depended on the diocese for the purchase of the vehicles. The diocese had, on the other hand, still to rely on outside help for this.

It was also during Ndingi's time that St Joseph's Seminary was opened in November 1980. Today it is a major contributor to the population of young Seminarians in the major seminary. Two major hospitals opened their doors to the public: one in Kaplong with a capacity of 220 beds, training facilities for lab technicians, enrolled nurses and enrolled midwives and Mercy Hospital with 80 beds. Community healthcare was also given priority and enabled many in remote places to get quality healthcare services.

Ndingi also started a process of Africanizing the Church in the Catholic Diocese of Nakuru; a task performed with tact and sensitivity. Some of the European priests who still operate in the diocese and who were there at the time recall that Ndingi would appoint Kenyan priests to parishes run by Europeans and make them understudies of the missionaries. But in so doing he also created what they believe was a good camaraderie among the clergy in Nakuru.

Indigenization in other places was beginning to create

some problems. Africans wanted to run their own affairs. The necessity of missionaries was being questioned with some people believing that they had outlived their usefulness. Rev John Gatu, Moderator of the Presbyterian Church of East Africa, was the first to express, in 1971, the idea that missionaries were no longer needed when he said, "The present missionary movement is a hindrance to the selfhood of the Church." Gatu was to remark that the obvious assumption of the enthusiastic missionary of the 19th century, that the African had no history and therefore no religion, made him denigrate the African past and impose on Africans the 'European present' clothed in the European religious garb of the day.[4]

Missionaries found themselves in a quandary in the early seventies. Comments made about them were openly denigrating. Some called them "necessary evils" but even distinguished scholars like Prof John Mbiti were of the view that their work in Kenya was, to put it mildly, over.

But Ndingi, while agreeing with the anachronism of missionaries in a new Kenya still accepted the idea that the Church in CDN must continue to welcome missionaries. Those already there were welcome, he suggested, and new ones like the Comboni Fathers, fleeing Uganda at the time, Holy Ghost Fathers, Fidei Donum priests as well as Kiltegan and Mill Hill priests were also welcome.

If there was something that the bishop acknowledged and respected about the missionaries it was their selflessness and their dedication to duty:

> Despite their educational and cultural background and their lack of knowledge of Africa, the early missionaries made a tremendous impact. Not only did they preach Christian religion,

---

[4] Gatu John, *Joyfully Christian, Truly African.*

but they also started primary, secondary and trade schools, teacher training colleges and hospitals...I would like to salute these men and women who so unselfishly shared their lives and worked with us and revealed to us the unknown God whom our ancestors had worshipped under a tree and for whom they built shrines.[5]

At the same time Ndingi proceeded to promote the diocesan priesthood. As Fr Newman observed, he went along with the setting up of the Commission on Africanisation, of which he was a member, more so to draw the attention of the expatriate missionaries to the urgency of this problem and the need to secure Kenyan staff for the various parishes.

Ndingi was also very supportive of the local Sisterhood. Some of the decisions he took with regard to this matter may have been seen as a bit controversial. For instance, the Little Sisters Novitiate in Bahati was promoted as if it were a Diocesan Congregation. While respecting their autonomy, he could, as Fr Newman put it, "make requests which they found difficult to turn down." But as we will see later, this is in keeping with the man's character. If he believed in an idea, he would go along with it no matter what others said.

Ndingi also established a tribunal which handled the more obvious cases of invalidity of marriage. Ndingi himself was the sole judge. The tribunal was called '*Ad hoc Marriage Tribunal*' and dealt with matters ranging from ratification to nullification of marriages.

One of his biggest milestones in Nakuru was the diocesan Synod, an idea first mooted by a European priest, Fr Fintan Byrne, in Molo one December morning in 1981. This was to

---
[5]St Patrick's missions magazine, March 1982. Article by Bishop Ndingi.

## Into a political hotbed

be a first in this part of the world. The only other precedent for a synod in English speaking Africa was in Lilongwe Malawi. Ndingi convinced that the synod was critical to his evangelisation and the need to hold the families together, chose, "The Christian Family" as the theme of the synod.

# CHAPTER TEN

## *Tempest in Rift Valley*

The early and mid seventies were characterised by the fever of impending political change. Mzee Jomo Kenyatta was getting old and frail and succession politics were beginning to occupy centre stage. A question over whether the constitution should be changed was beginning to arouse passion among politicians.

The Church then took a dilatory approach to these matters preferring that politicians sort them out instead of the Church loudly adding its voice to the issue. The voice of the Catholic Church then was seen as, at worst, non-existent and at best, pretty muted. The Church had, strangely, maintained a low public profile on contentious issues even though, when it did speak, it was taken quite seriously. It could not be compared to the Presbyterian Church of East Africa and the Church of the Province of Kenya which were highly outspoken and visible when it came to political matters.

The CPK's assault was led by Dr Henry Okullu who was the Bishop of Maseno South, Rt Rev David Gitari, Bishop of Mt Kenya diocese and Bishop Alexander Kipsang Muge of the Eldoret diocese. The Rev Timothy Njoya was the most vocal in the Presbyterian church to the extent that he was labelled a *"subversive cleric."* It is right to say that in the absence of an active opposition party, these clergymen had taken the role of the opposition party in the country.

Coupled with a few other clerics, these voices drowned that of the Catholic Church in what many saw as unsettling. But if the seeming silence of the Church then was loud, anyone who mistook it for docility was later to get a rude awakening. Many, however, wondered why a Church with millions of followers was afraid to be seen at the forefront of social justice and why the role of defending the voiceless seemed to have been completely taken up by other churches.

Those who were wondering did not have long to do so. For the voice of the Church was to be heard in deafening decibels across the land quite soon.

In the 1980s, the government decided to change the system of voting in the general election and in KANU nominations. Instead of the secret ballot, the 1988 election would be conducted through the queuing system. KANU was the ruling party, nay, the only legal party then since the country was a *de facto* one-party state which after former President Daniel Moi's ascent to power in 1978, spread its wings and received a lot of support through seminars and campaigns. In just a few years KANU became so strong that by the 1980s it had become a political monstrosity.

Some equated it to George Orwell's *Big Brother* (1984): omnipresent, ruthless and invasive. If one fell out with the party, they were literally crushed. Many were those who upon being grilled by the KANU disciplinary committee, broke down in tears and anguished for days and then had to agonisingly watch as they were shredded bit by bit by the party apparatchiks.

To be thrown out of KANU was to have one's livelihood cut, to become nothing. Those were the days when politicians used to compete as to who was more 'KANU' than the other. One politician, famously said that if his veins were cut, only

KANU not just blood, would flow. Some politicians walked the streets with what some people cheekily called 'KANU-metres' to gauge the level of one's loyalty to the party. The KANU membership card was a requirement much as a national identity card was. Every person of voting age was, *ipso facto*, a member of KANU. Those who occupied lofty perches within the party from the branch to national level wielded fearsome influence in society. Some were loathed, others feared and still others admired. KANU, as they used to say, was the father and mother of all. It was a political obelisk that awed and dumbfounded all those who came into contact with it.

The queue voting system, as many saw it, was designed to ensure that only those favourable to the ruling party got elected. While selling the idea, the government had argued that it was a safer method of voting since it left little room for fighting during campaigns and the elections. Exactly how it was supposed to achieve this was still a matter of conjecture to many. But suffice it to say that at a time when the name KANU sent shivers down the spines of many, it would have been suicidal for one to be seen to be against a candidate favoured by the President or, so to speak, the government. The government knew this and, though never spoke loudly, many knew it was KANU's way of arm-twisting the public to vote for its preferred candidates.

The new method of election also decreed that whoever attained 70 per cent of the vote at the nomination level would be declared winner. This triggered intense debate with those opposed to it arguing that it was open to abuse and, at worst, it was incompatible with the country's constitution. A cabal of politicians who had already distinguished themselves as fighters for justice raved and ranted against this system. The clergymen fulminated against it at the pulpits and the general public just watched and listened, careful not to break into any applause for what they saw as a fight gallantly put up by a few brave people and the risk of being labelled anti-Nyayo or anti-KANU.

For during this time, KANU was the alpha and omega and the public grudgingly accepted this. The Catholic Church's Justice and Peace Commission and the Church of the Province of Kenya were later to say in a joint statement:

> Fear was the order of the day. Before long, that fear became a new culture in the national life; the culture of fear. The institutions that dared criticise the government were intimidated and some succumbed to silence.

As the debate raged and the clerics added their voice, the Catholic Church, like a super substitute who comes in to change the course of the game made its grand entry into the fray. The Catholic Church usually made its views known through the powerful Kenya Episcopal Conference which normally released a statement signed by all the country's Catholic bishops and which often was taken seriously enough by the media to make newspaper headlines. When it thundered, its voice was like that of Jeremiah pronouncing doom on the apostates. But this voice never seemed to thunder often.

However, in September 1987, the voice of Ndingi, starting out as what could have been a loud cry in the wilderness of shrivelled and mortified hearts, rose above the seeming silence to issue a statement that rocked the very foundations of the establishment. Ndingi, the Bishop of the Catholic Diocese of Nakuru had been invited to Ufungamano House near the University of Nairobi to address a predominantly university audience. He chose the topic "Religion and Politics." Fielding questions to the audience, the issue of the queue voting arose. Ndingi did not waste time in condemning it. "I was opposed to it from the start," he said in a voice both defiant and fearless, "and I am still opposed to it," he told an interviewer singling out the 70 per cent requirement.

This immediately made headlines the following day. The authoritative weekly newspaper then, The *Weekly Review*, had Ndingi on the cover under the heading, "The Catholic Voice" and the newspapers ran articles outlining the Catholic Church's opposition to the new system. It was not lost on many that the views in question were not contained in a pastoral letter or in a statement from and by the Kenya Episcopal Conference, nor did it surprise many that Ndingi's lone voice had been labelled "The Catholic Voice." It was as if it was what many had been waiting for.

Ndingi's pronouncement was important in many ways. First, he was the chairman of the Kenya Episcopal Conference, which had, the previous year issued a formal statement on the matter but which did not have the seismic effect that his pronouncement had had. Two, while the Presbyterian Church of East Africa and Church of the Province of Kenya clerics usually spoke in their individual capacities and were taken on by politicians as individuals, Catholics then rarely took an individual stand on a matter. The Catholic Church was known to speak in one voice and often issued pastoral letters to explain its position on various issues. Such a letter was usually authored by the bishops after a meeting and signed by all of them. The effect was that the Church attained the figure of a colossus that always spoke in one mighty voice. Was Ndingi then breaking out of the mould? Those who had followed his utterances in the past were convinced that what they were seeing was just a shade of the man's true colours.

In the past, he had made utterances that attracted immense

attention. Shortly after the failed 1982 coup, he made a statement that was seen as the Church's reaction to the events of the time. "The Church does not exist to bolster any regime, tolerate any regime, or oppose any regime" he told the AMECEA bishops in a homily at the Holy Family Basilica in August 1982. In a brave pronouncement at a time when political temperatures were scorchingly high, Ndingi went on, "We (the Church) belong to the apostolate of truth and courage, of pity and healing, of unselfishness and love. We belong to all regimes that promote and support such values. The Church is critical of all regimes that do not support and promote truth and courage."[1]

At that time the Catholic Church was being criticised for not coming out clearly to condemn the coup plotters. But Ndingi defended the Church with lucidity and authority that made those criticising it think again. While the Church may have become identified with the social and political set-up, he said, it should also make it clear to the civil authority that its dimensions were not temporal but eternal. "While we support projects aimed at improving the human lot, we look primarily to a horizon beyond the visible, the tangible, the temporary."

When he then spoke on the issue of queue voting system, few expected him to mince his words even though his position on the matter would be misconstrued for disloyalty. Though there was nothing more feared than being labelled disloyal, Ndingi appeared unbothered about what the government would think of his statement. While restating the principal spiritual aims of the Christian, Ndingi suggested that Christians must take a more active role when the secular authority failed to keep to certain values. "If we are to do away with corruption, bribes, crooked and devious ways of acquiring property, we must be

---

[1] *Mwananchi Magazine*, August 1991.

ready to suffer, to be thought of as fools," he thundered, "a religious leader must act as God's prophet, especially with regard to human and people's rights, and freedom of conscience."

Ndingi then had no problem with KANU's choice as a political party or its selection of candidates. But he argued that the 70 per cent rule disenfranchised many Kenyans because KANU was the only party and they had no recourse had they felt that the ruling party's rules were unfair.

Only the previous year, Ndingi had risen up to add his voice to the debate on the voting system, joining a chorus of other leaders with similar views. He was roundly condemned by politicians, among whom was the man who had helped him set up Catholic schools when he was Education Secretary, Moses Mudavadi. Mudavadi was then the Minister for Local Government and one of Moi's staunchest defenders. As was the tradition those days, one's loyalty was also measured by how loudly one condemned those opposing the government or attacking the president in whatever way. So Mudavadi reserved some of the harshest words for Ndingi calling him "a lost sheep that needs to be put on the right track."

But if the politicians thought that Ndingi was acting alone then, they missed out on the Catholic consensus on the issue. For shortly afterwards, the Catholic bishops submitted a memorandum to the President which also sparked off a heated debate. The memorandum expressed concern that some politicians claimed that the power of the party was paramount, exceeding even that of parliament. "The suggestion is made that anyone who says otherwise is disloyal to Your Excellency and anti-Nyayo," it read.

The memorandum, presented personally to the president,

also appealed to him to reconsider the new voting method. "We feel that we would be failing in our duty if we did not draw your attention to the danger of divisiveness inherent in the proposed system," they outlined, "we appeal on behalf of others who would risk becoming marked men and women by this public manner of voting. We can envisage situations where professional businessmen and even the humblest worker would be made to compromise their means of livelihood or abstain from exercising their right to vote." The bishops lamented that there was a certain inadequacy of dialogue in the country and called for further debate on the issue before a final decision was made.

The memorandum was soft, civil and firm. But this did not prevent overzealous politicians from attacking it. Assistant Minister for Co-operative Development, then Archbishop Stephen Ondiek, wondered why the bishops had chosen to oppose attempts by the government to make changes meant to benefit Kenyans while the government had never opposed any changes in church organisations. The powerful KANU Secretary-General, Burudi Nabwera, accused the bishops of dishonesty for giving copies of the memorandum to the press adding that the matter should have been kept secret.

Shortly after his University of Nairobi address, Ndingi took up the issue further the following year. He issued a coruscating statement on the voting system, copies of which were amply distributed to the media. The statement made it clear that the bishop was putting forward his views on the matter as a registered voter. The statement was seen as the boldest reaction yet from a Catholic bishop on this matter. Ndingi said in the statement that as a registered voter in Nakuru district, he had been among approximately 150,000 fellow registered voters who had had no opportunity to exercise their constitutional right to vote for a candidate of their choice to parliament because of the new system.

"In Nakuru district, which has a total registered electorate of about 208,000, only 58,977 (about 28%) got an opportunity to express their preference in the national elections. It now appears increasingly evident that these MPs will be asked very soon to decide in parliament whether or not I should ever again have a say in the selection of my representative in parliament."

The statement said that removing the secret ballot system "threatens a very serious cutback of democracy in our country [sic]." Ndingi took issue with the fact that the KANU regime was leaving no room for debate on the matter and that it seemed to have completely made up its mind to implement the new system. He particularly took issue with a statement by a KANU hawk, Shariff Nassir, who was Assistant Minister for National Guidance and Political Affairs who had said that the secret ballot would be replaced by queueing, *wapende wasipende* (whether people like it or not.)

Nassir's view was that KANU was becoming totalitarian and that his statement had made it clear that any national debate on the matter was a waste of time. Nassir represented the worst of KANU's strong headedness. He was quoted in the media around the same time as saying, "When KANU members decide to do something, it will be done. Those who are not KANU members cannot stop them and it will be done whether they like it or not."

The defence of an unpopular system underlined the arrogance of KANU officials at the time and this set off Ndingi. Nassir brooked neither dissent nor argument. "What form of debate can there be when a spokesman of the Ministry of National Guidance threatens MPs with disciplinary action if they voice an opinion in favour of the secret ballot system? Surely, even as KANU members, the MPs should be allowed to voice their true opinions. What else does the word debate mean?" wondered Ndingi.

According to Ndingi, the only true form of debate would be to allow MPs plenty of time to return to their constituencies and hold genuine public meetings with their people "where they can be truly briefed as to what the real wishes of the majority of their constituents are."

The bishop asked KANU to first investigate allegations of rigging that the new system had already perfected in previous nominations and decried the fact that KANU did not seem to be bothered by the claims of rigging. "I would have hoped that the KANU hierarchy would be concerned, not just with the fact of those allegations, but with whether they were true or not. I would have hoped to hear that KANU had instituted public inquiries into the truth or otherwise of such allegations." But according to the bishops, the allegations had been totally ignored "as though the persons making them were non-persons."

Ndingi concluded his statement by attempting to rally the nation behind him and sending a warning to the system that his views represented those of many others. "Though I speak in the first person in most of this statement," he wrote, "I have no doubt that what I say represents the views of very many of my fellow Kenyan citizens."

The last paragraph of the statement is what startled and annoyed politicians because of its brashness and audacity:

> I pray that God...will direct our government, and KANU, to give adequate attention to these views; otherwise, they may win the battle and outlaw the secret ballot, but at what cost? At the cost of further alienating the majority of thinking Kenyans from a party and government that is increasingly intolerant of the people's views and wishes. I genuinely fear for the future of true democracy in our country and I appeal to our leaders to consider very seriously the path they seem determined to follow *"watu wapende wasipende."*

Such a candid letter was virtually unknown in an era when people would disappear, get detained, get sacked for holding different political views or die in mysterious circumstances. Further, it was quite unlike the Catholic Church to come out so strongly on the issue. But because it was not done under the aegis of the Kenya Episcopal Conference, it was easy to isolate Ndingi and attack his person while appearing to leave out the larger Catholic church.

There then followed a barrage of criticism with every politician trying to outdo the other in their condemnation of the prelate. But as Ndingi had said in the letter, he represented the views of the silent many who could not voice their concerns for fear of being targeted by the dreaded KANU machinery.

A flurry of letters in support of what he had said followed. St Mulumba Catholic Church, which at the time was under Fr Ndikaru wa Teresia, another thorn in the flesh of the government, was among the first to express support for the bishop. Its Justice and Peace Commission called for the scrapping of the queue voting system and urged the bishop to continue speaking fearlessly on this matter. St Patrick's Catholic Church, Eldama Ravine; Convent of Our Lady of Lourdes, Nyahururu; St Theresa's Gekano Girl's Secondary School, Kisii; St Paul's Catholic Chapel, Nairobi and the Diocese of Kitui were among those who wrote urging the bishop to continue with the fight against the new voting system.

Those within the Church felt that Catholics, through the fearlessness of Ndingi, were at last standing up to be counted. They felt that since their faithfuls could not speak out freely, they were grateful to the one good man who dared take the bull by the horns. One letter sent to Ndingi after his statement was particularly telling:

> From where I stand, I see your statement as a very important one and one that is necessary for the advancement of the Church. If no such voice were to be heard from the Church leaders, it would be sinful on the part of the Church. May God give you the courage to continue giving this witness.

The letter came from Fr Christy Burke of the Saint Paul's Catholic Chapel, University of Nairobi chaplaincy.

As support poured in, so did condemnation. If the politicians thought Ndingi would relent, they were wrong. He had no such ideas. He took every opportunity to lambast politicians and he attracted the media wherever he went. Wisdom, he told the politicians who were criticising him, was not an exclusive reserve of politicians. Other Kenyans were endowed with it and the Church leaders had "a right to air their views."

Though the KANU regime proceeded to force the queue voting system, the public, Ndingi and the other clergymen who had opposed it, were vindicated by the sheer number of cases of rigging and irregularities reported following the general election. Some politicians who were for the system, or did not condemn it for fear of reprisals, actually witnessed situations where the person with the shortest queue was declared the winner and because there was no evidence later to bear out that fact, the matter rested there. Many of them became casualties of a system they so pusillanimously condoned.

Nevertheless, Ndingi continued with his outspokenness, forwarding to the KANU Review Committee a report from the Christians of Catholic Diocese of Nakuru on the elections, which was not exactly flattering to the ruling party. The report stopped short of calling for the adoption of a multiparty system, but more importantly emphasised the need for national dialogue to chart out the political future of the country.

In many ways, Nakuru was seen as a hotbed of politics. It did not help matters that it was the home district of the then President Daniel arap Moi and that Ndingi was actually fomenting political dissent right in his backyard.

Moi's minions continued campaigning against Ndingi, some calling him names and others suggesting that he should even be jailed. But what the politicians did not know was that Ndingi was an indefatigable fighter. On 2nd August 1990, he released another statement, this time suggesting that the President must listen more to the people and that he must bring to an end the prevailing situation where some people appeared to enjoy impunity and immunity even when that was hurting the country. He criticized those who had attempted to stymie debate on the voting system and on the political changes going on in the country. "When people whisper their opinions in bars they are called rumour-mongers but when they speak openly for all to hear, some of our political leaders resort to authoritarian threats."

In a feather-ruffling statement, Ndingi suggested that the president and his advisers were capable of making mistakes. This was at a time when the president and his advisers were thought to be infallible; too powerful to be challenged.

Ndingi took issue with Moi's support for particular

candidates during the election, saying in no uncertain terms, "It does not seem right and proper for our Head of State to support a particular candidate (at least in public) during elections. Furthermore, the language used on such instances seems improper and unbecoming." Then he crossed the taboo line: that of advising the president:

> Perhaps our president should leave certain public statements to his ministers and other senior government officials so that we are free then to respond to them, if and when necessary without feeling that we are criticising the man who holds the highest responsibility in our land.

Was there a way of stilling this voice? Apparently not. Even as the political establishment seemed intent on rubbishing the bishop, his star was rising not just locally but also in the Holy See. For on 26th June 1989, Ndingi received a letter from Cardinal Agostino Casaroli, the Holy See's Secretary of State, communicating the decision by Pope John Paul II to appoint Ndingi as a member of the Pontifical Council for Social Communications. A similar letter was to follow, this time from the president of the Pontifical Commission for the Means of Social Communications, Archbishop John J. Foley.

If there was one thing that seemed to irk the bishop, it was keeping mum when things were not right. He expected his Church to be at the forefront of justice and peace issues and he was not going to be ashamed of taking up this role. He believed that if the Church did not speak then it would lose valuable opportunities to lead from the front and it also risked losing the faith of its followers.

"From my own experience, once people who suffer from one or another form of oppression know the Church is fully behind them, they speak their mind, stand their ground and politicians listen," he told bishops in Nairobi in August, 1989.

He wondered loudly why the Church was sometimes timid in exposing social and political injustices.

"It is unfortunate that very few of our local priests and religious leaders take up cases of justice and peace. Many of them are afraid to take a stand for and in defence of people's rights. Consequently, courses on justice and peace, human rights and liberation from evil in any form or nature are a must at our theological institutions, houses of formation, spiritual centers and pastoral institutions."

And so he never missed any opportunity to lash out at injustice. In June 1990, when the voices of dissent started to openly challenge the government, some politicians, notably then cabinet minister Elijah Mwangale, proposed that the government revives detention without trial in Kenya. Ndingi rose up against Mwangale in a dramatic way. In a press statement, issued on June 20, 1990 Ndingi asserted that resorting to detention without trial would signify the breakdown of law and order.

"Furthermore, it connotes the inability of political power to restore the status quo without use of extreme measures, which, ultimately may be classified as a weakness," he said.

Then he rounded on Mwangale[2] wondering if he would have advocated for the same in 1975 when he chaired the parliamentary probe into the murder of J.M Kariuki, "Now, however, he calls for these measures with impunity," he said, "Does he have the assent of the *Vox populi-Vox Dei* (Voice of the people is the voice of God)? Does he give the axiom its correct interpretation and take account of a well formed, an informed and knowledgeable conscience?"

---

[2] Elijah Mwangale chaired the parliamentary inquiry into the death of politician J.M Kariuki who was murdered in the 1970s. He came through as a fearless non-conformist

Ndingi's outspokenness contrasted sharply with the calm and modulated voice of his superior, His Eminence Michael Cardinal Maurice Otunga. Otunga never was as outspoken as Ndingi. But he lent support to all that Ndingi said and respected the fact that Ndingi had taken it as a key part of his pastoral duties to speak on social injustices based on the Church's social doctrine. In fact, Cardinal Otunga was known more for his primacy and his serenity than his utterances. Ndingi was variously referred to as the Voice of the Church. Others saw him as a radical. But he resented being labelled a radical or a controversial prelate. The things he spoke about, he insisted, were the very ones many people wanted to speak out on but did not have the right forum. On June 23, 1985, Ndingi sought to clear the air about his so called radicalism, "I do not think I deserve to be called a 'radical' or a 'controversial' clergyman. I have been lucky this far to have been able to live a quiet life as a priest and bishop. I have enjoyed the support of fellow bishops, fellow priests, religious and laity."[3]

Ndingi's outspokenness got into the public domain because he was mainly speaking on issues of interest to the entire nation – politics. But what many may have ignored was the fact that when it came to defending an issue, the bishop never shied away from a good fight.

## Fighting the mandarins

The development projects started by the Catholic Church were arousing quite some passion in some districts. Some churches were opposed to a strong Catholic presence and the influence on the people. The politicians felt that the Church was taking

---

[3] See, *Kenya Times*, June 23 1985

their place in the leadership structure and they therefore started opposing individual priests and placing hurdles in the way of the development of some projects even though they were meant to benefit the local people. Some of the development projects were concentrated in an area called Kipsaraman, spearheaded by Fr Sean O'Laoire. Fr Sean was a fearless, determined man, who the politicians disliked immensely. He was accused of inciting the people and posing a security threat.

On November 31, 1984, Ndingi received a call from Hezekiah Oyugi, the then powerful Provincial Commissioner (PC), Rift Valley. Oyugi told the bishop that Fr Sean had to be removed from the area and from Kenya with immediate effect. "He is a security risk," Oyugi said. Oyugi's word was law and he had the ear of the president anytime. For him to express such a wish was a pointer to the official view held by the government on the matter. Nevertheless, Ndingi responded with a firm no. He told him that as far as he was concerned, there was no valid reason for the PC's request and therefore, he could not act on it. If on the other hand, he told him, the government had valid reasons, security or political, it could go ahead and deport the priest.

Fr Sean's problems did not disappear after Ndingi's support. The politicians continued agitating for the priest's deportation but Ndingi stood firm and resisted the pressure. On 1st January the following year, Ndingi called the PC and repeated the same stance on the priest. He also communicated the same to the Vicars General, Fr Peter Coyle and Fr Eddie Lolar, St Patrick's regional superior.

Between May and June 1984, the local chief was so harsh that he was caning and mistreating people as well as interfering with development projects approved by the district development committees. Fr Sean reported this to the president and got the locals to sign a statement supporting the claim. While the people were happy that their priest was standing up for them, the administration was not. Fr Sean was threatened physically, assaulted and false accusations levelled against him. In January 1985, the DC, Mr Philemon Mwaisaka, called Ndingi and asked him to transfer Fr Sean. The bishop once again refused. He stood by Fr Sean every inch of the way until the administration and the politicians relented.

Soon after, Ndingi and the Catholic Church took on the government on the issue of family planning. In the 1980s the government started a campaign on family planning. The reasoning behind this was that a leaner family would be better provided for and the government therefore started encouraging couples to visit family planning centres for artificial contraceptives. But the Church was fiercely opposed to this method of contraception. However, it was careful not to be seen as openly contradicting government policy and therefore urged its followers to seek natural family planning methods acceptable to the Church.

But in November 1984, the Catholic bishops led by Maurice Cardinal Otunga, issued a public protest in the form of advertisements in the daily newspapers against a number of family planning camps in the country. The camps were already performing surgical sterilisations on rural women and had been approved by the Ministry of Health. These were conducted jointly by the Lions Clubs of Nakuru and the Giants Group. The bishops then described the programme as a mutilation of the reproductive organs which was against natural law and appealed to Kenyans to reject the procedures and stop visiting the camps. The government came out fighting and accused the Church of trying to shoot down its developmental goals. The bishop of Eldoret, John Njenga, had to clarify that the Church was not opposed to family planning but was only against the use of artificial contraception. The debate appeared to die but Ndingi was not convinced that family planning was wholly about development.

On March 26, 1988, Ndingi outlined the position of the Catholic church with respect to contraception in an address delivered at the Asumbi Teachers' College. While terming the government's policy of family planning as genuine and necessary, he pointed out that the government was succumbing to pressure from "external agencies." These agencies, he said, "would wave the banner of 'Kenya's soaring birth-rate' to further their own ends and eventually find a market for contraceptive technology. Meanwhile, we continue to be used as a 'dumping ground' for dangerous medication, considered unsuitable for use in the developed world."

Though this was only reported at a lower scale compared to the bishop's earlier stances on political issues, it nearly changed the course of the debate from whether family planning was necessary to whether the government was not imperiling its citizenry by advocating for artificial contraception.

"We have a situation where millions of women in Africa, Asia and South America are being asked to accept the unacceptable," he told the teachers. "Birth control devices and drugs which are considered unsafe for women in the United States are being distributed in the Third World on a Massive scale."

Then Ndingi took on the manufacturers and distributors, "The information labels are often removed when supplies of contraceptive pills and injections are made available to the developing countries so that both doctors and patients are generally uninformed on the risks involved."

Ndingi saw the push for family planning as an idea being pursued by foreigners at the expense of the ignorant rural Masses. The artificial methods on offer contradicted the Church's teachings on family planning and the Pope's encyclical, *Humanae Vitae*, on the issue.

Ndingi's voice was to remain loud on this matter for a long time to come. In fact, when much later he became the Archbishop of Nairobi Diocese, his opposition to the use of condoms became his most defining feature.

# CHAPTER ELEVEN

## *In the eye of the storm*

For people residing in some parts of the Rift Valley, the period 1991-1992 was a time of living dangerously. At that time ethnic clashes had broken out around Kipkelion, Olenguruoni, Molo and some parts of Bomet. The government preferred calling them land clashes, attempting to convince the masses that what was happening there were just simple clashes but there was more than met the eye. Houses were being torched and people were being killed senselessly. Neighbour was rising against neighbour and communities where people had lived peacefully for years became veritable tinder boxes. In spite of this, the government still wanted people to believe that the clashes were about land. In fact, the term tribal clashes disappeared from the media and the softer 'land-clashes' became the defining term for the atrocity happening in the Rift Valley. It was largely seen as a Kikuyu-Kalenjin affair where two tribes had turned against each other with dreadful consequences.

Two things made this conundrum puzzling. First, it was coming at a time when the clamour for multipartysm was at its peak. KANU's hegemony, as a political party that had ruled the country since independence, was being fiercely challenged by a rabid opposition. The supporters of Forum for Restoration of Democracy (FORD) were mainly Luos, Luhyas and Kikuyus and some of them resided in the Rift Valley. To ensure that they did not vote, they had to be uprooted from the province.

Second, there was what was seen as government torpor in dealing with the problem. When the clashes first broke out, the government did nothing to stop them. In some cases it was claimed that the raiders were receiving police protection and even as the fighting continued no one was getting arrested for the atrocity. Some believed that ethnic-cleansing was at work.

As the atrocity continued, the allegations that some of those actively involved were members of KANU, were rife. In just five days, twenty thousand people had been displaced and were now gathered in open areas requesting for intervention from the government.

On the Sunday morning of November 3, 1991, a group of armed raiders had invaded farms belonging to non-Kalenjins in Kokwet, Chepkechei and Mtaragon areas, set houses ablaze, shot people with arrows and raped women. Consequently, the displaced families ran away and sought refuge at a nearby school, leaving their farms at the mercy of raiders and looters.

Sitting in the bishopric house in Nakuru, Ndingi received the news with shock. A number of priests, stunned at what they had seen, took the bishop through the entire episode, giving him a blow by blow account of what had happened. Desperation, anger and helplessness permeated the atmosphere.

Ndingi reclined in his seat and listened much more carefully. The priests who knew him well also knew that he usually acted on his feet when a burning issue was brought to his attention. But on this morning, he just sat dazed and listened like one in a trance. Then he took out his pen and started jotting. As the moral disgust of the entire problem receded in Ndingi's mind, its political and historical contours became visible.

"Something has to be done," he told one of the priests, "we

must make the whole world aware of the goings on. The Church must play its role."

Unbeknown to the priests, Ndingi's statement that "something has to be done" was the start of a long and bruising moral crusade against what was to clearly emerge as one of the biggest crimes against humanity to be committed in that part of the country.

That very day, the Catholic priests of Nakuru Diocese crafted a strongly worded statement on the clashes, calling on the government to protect the lives and property of the communities living in the Rift Valley.

"These are people who acquired their land legally and are ready to be issued with title deeds...their future is now unclear to them. Though they have been promised security and a return to their land they feel that this guarantee is too little; too late," the statement read.

The priests wondered if the government was trying to balkanize the nation. "The torching of houses and property appear to have been carefully planned and orchestrated. In Kunyak, eyewitnesses stated that KANU officials were actively involved...there is no doubt that these events have caused great damage to trust and confidence among different ethnic groups. Is this majimboism in action?"

The statement was endorsed by Ndingi as the bishop. It did not, however, make the screaming headlines that other stories from Ndingi had previously done. Still, it was a handy warning shot and a declaration that the Catholic Church was not about to take a backseat while people were dying and their houses being burnt.

The clashes had now spread to areas bordering Kisumu, affecting three dioceses: Kisumu, Nakuru and Eldoret. The bishops of the three dioceses, Archbishop Zacheaus Okoth of Kisumu, Ndingi and Cornelius Korir of Eldoret, Archbishop John Njenga of Mombasa, John Njue of Embu and Father Ndikaru wa Teresia, the editor of *Mwananchi Magazine* got together and visited the affected areas. They were horrified at what they saw.

Hordes of people walking along the God-forsaken roads of Olengurueni and Molo, stunned them. Dead bodies lay strewn along the road and warriors armed with arrows were spoiling for war. They saw cows, mooing with the pain of unmilked udders; heard the agonised bleat of goats which, like their human owners, had been displaced from the familiarity of their pens; saw lost children crying for their parents, some unaware that their parents had been killed or seriously wounded and they saw the charred remains of what used to be peaceful homes; the scorched expanses of what used to be fecund earth. They beheld the unrepentant, blood-thirsty faces of the killers of Molo.

The picture was horrifying. Archbishop Njue could not contain himself and he shed tears. Njue, was so enraged that, as those who were there recall, it was difficult to know if the tears were out of pain or anger. Amidst sobs, he took out his camera and took some pictures of the warriors armed with arrows. He had underestimated the tempestuous nature of the moment because at that point, some young men approached them menacingly.

"Why did you take our pictures?" one of them asked.

Brandishing pangas, they demanded that the bishop gives them the camera. Bishop Njue hesitated and the men closed in. Sensing serious trouble, Ndingi implored Njue to acquiesce.

"Let's not cause a commotion by taking photos," Ndingi pleaded with a frustrated Njue. "These people can even kill us."

They took the camera and unspooled the film, then furiously stomped on it.

Bishop Njenga recalls seeing planes dropping arrows in the area, which were then hastily collected by the locals. For some time, he thought he was wrong but it dawned on him that the situation was not as it had been reported in the media. People were not fully aware of what was going on in the Rift Valley. The whole issue had been made to look like a case of simple land clashes between warring tribes. But there was more to it. This was a war by one heavily backed set of people against another unarmed, hapless lot. It was a war full of fire and rage and in many ways, devoid of sense.

After this scaring episode, the bishops continued with their fact-finding mission. At one point they met an old woman on the road and stopped the car.

"Where are you going?" Bishop Njenga asked the old, haggard and scared woman.

"I don't know?" she replied.

The bishops consulted and decided to take the woman in their car. They went all the way to Olenguruoni parish where they left the woman under the care of the parish priest.

"We as pastors must speak out," they proclaimed, quoting the book of Luke (19:40) "I tell you, if these keep silent the stones will cry out."

Getting back to the Kenya Catholic Secretariat, they crafted a statement challenging the government to break its silence and bring the clashes to an end. Then they cobbled together a collection of other bishops from other denominations with the intention of seeking an appointment with the president.

In Nairobi, they called the Head of the Civil Service, Prof Mbithi and asked him to arrange an appointment for them to see the president. Prof Mbithi was reluctant, probably sensing that the bishops were up to their rabble-rousing activities again.

"If we do not see the president today, we will demonstrate at the Holy Family Basilica tomorrow," they told him.

Mbithi realised that things were serious and that the clerics perhaps meant every word they said. He hastily organised a meeting for the bishops. All the ecumenical bishops met the president at State House that day at six in the evening. The meeting, Bishop Njenga recalls, was tense.

After Archbishop Okoth read the statement prepared by the bishops, Archbishop Njenga addressed the president. "Your Excellency, people are dying, we saw planes dropping arrows in the area and the situation is serious."

Moi hit the roof. "Bishop Njenga, I think you are exaggerating," he thundered. "The pilots you are referring to are Kikuyus. How can they drop arrows that would kill their people?" he asked.

"Your Excellency, given money they will do anything, even if they are Kikuyus."

Things were hotting up. The meeting was tense. The bishops were angry. The president was also annoyed at the audacity of the bishops. Silence descended on the room; no one wanted to speak and no one knew who would speak next and what they would say. The president fixed his gaze on the bishops.

All of a sudden one of the bishops rose to speak. He began to thank the president for the good deeds he had done for the country, pouring profuse praise on the Head of State.

"Your Excellency, I came here to thank you for the help you have given my church," one bishop said, "we have been able to do a lot with your generous contributions."

Another one would thank the president for helping his son

get a scholarship and suddenly a few others chimed in with praises and panegyrics. The whole course of the meeting changed. Moi sat there enjoying the whole drama and the sudden *volte face* some of the bishops had made to change the course of the entire conversation. What had been, only a few minutes ago, a matter of grave national and public concern, was turned into a circus of praises. The Catholic bishops were seemingly isolated as the others chanted praises for the president and ignored the topic for which they had sought an appointment. Needless to say, when the meeting ended, some of the bishops were assailed by a fierce sense of betrayal, a feeling that the meeting they had so painstakingly sought and issued threats over had miserably failed.

Perhaps unbeknown to some of the bishops was that the coterie of bishops was divided down the middle. There were those who were fierce loyalists and there were those who were genuinely searching for justice. The former are the ones who changed the course of the conversation.

Bishop Ndingi was crestfallen. He felt betrayed by some of his colleagues and as they left State House, he was almost in tears. He knew then that nothing would be done, that the president had not taken them seriously and that the appointment had come to nought.

In the following three months, the clashes continued. A litany of anguish and woe loomed large across a section of the kaleidoscope of Rift Valley.

Kamwaura area in Molo experienced some of the most vicious clashes with a hundred houses belonging to non-Kalenjins razed to the ground. About two thousand homeless and displaced people sought refuge in St John and Paul churches in Kamwaura. Eight of them were killed. In Elburgon area,

46 houses were burnt on March 16, 1992, while during the same period, a group of about thirty youngsters from the Kalenjin community started burning houses belonging to the non-Kalenjins. They were doing this while guarded by elders armed with bows and arrows. Over fifty houses were torched. On March 18, some houses were burned in Njoro area, some primary schools were shut down and several people were killed in an area called Larmudiac, near Egerton University.

Sensing that the clashes were not about to abate, Ndingi gathered his priests for a meeting. In the charged meeting, statistics on the death and suffering of the people of Rift Valley were put on the table. On the Feast of Saint Joseph on March 19, 1992, the priests and the bishop, once again released a statement expressing concern at the killings and destruction of property and just fell short of blaming the government for the violence.

"Our analysis leads us to conclude that there is reluctance among our political leaders to contain the situation and this reluctance depicts a certain lack of confidence in those empowered to guide and protect us."

Ndingi was so immersed and concerned at what was happening that he rarely wanted to spend time out of Nakuru. Later in that month he was invited to Nyeri for the silver jubilee of some nuns and he took this opportunity to enlighten other clergy of the bleak situation in Nakuru.

"Things are very bad there?" he responded. One priest described him as a distraught man whose concentration would sometimes waver to what must have been the plight of his people down at Nakuru. "His mind was not with us at all," recalls one bishop. After the function, one of his fellow bishops tried to persuade Ndingi to spend the night in Nyeri and travel to

Nakuru the following morning but he would hear none of it.

"No," he responded, " I have to go back. I have to be with my people. I cannot leave my people alone." And go back, he did.

During Easter of that year, the clashes reached their climax. More homes were burned, more people were killed and thousands of anguished and displaced people thronged churches for help. The government was sending no help to the many victims strewn all over church compounds in the area. To make matters worse, no government officials visited the area. Ndingi felt that matters were reaching intolerable levels and decided to take on the government personally, once again. He released a statement, this time written and signed by himself as the Bishop of the Diocese of Nakuru, squarely blaming the government for the clashes:

> How is it that, after so many assurances by the president that people can live anywhere and own property anywhere people continue to get displaced? As recently as 13th February, 1992, the president had assured people that anyone burning houses would be punished but houses continue to burn in Eldoret today and any policeman on duty in these clash torn areas who tries to defend the innocent and shoots or kills an attacker is transferred. How is it that nobody has been prosecuted for burning houses or shooting people with arrows? Our conclusion is that the government of Kenya – KANU government is behind the clashes.

This was followed by a documentation of all those killed and the places where the atrocities were committed.

The government did not do much in the way of exonerating itself. Around that time, the clamour for multiparty democracy had reached fever-pitch with the main opposition party, Forum for the Restoration of Democracy (FORD) presenting KANU with its toughest challenge yet. The KANU diehards continued threatening those who were seen to oppose KANU or embrace the opposition. "Those who do not sing the KANU song," a KANU politician proclaimed in public on February 27, 1992, "will be chased away."

By this time, Cardinal Otunga was getting increasingly wary of the situation. The government never really worried about him as the politicians knew him to be an extremely guarded clergyman who eschewed controversy. Whether they ignored him or just kept him at arms length was sometimes hard to tell. His manner contrasted sharply with that of Ndingi and other senior clergymen who were known to fly off the handle whenever they sensed injustice. The government sometimes praised him for his silence and sobriety.

But this time, the cardinal too could not keep quiet. On January 24, 1991, he invited Ndingi to his house in Nairobi. He was in a pensive mood and he went straight to the point. After voicing his distress at what was happening in the Rift Valley, he told the bishop: "We must do something to defend the people."

Ndingi agreed fully with the cardinal. For a moment, he was pleased that the cardinal had been moved into some sort of action by the tragedy unfolding in the country. But he also knew that "doing something to defend the people" also meant plunging headlong into the crisis and leading from the front. Did the cardinal have the guts to do this?

The encounter with the cardinal left Ndingi in some sort of confusion. He did not know where to place Otunga's outrage neither did he know how far Otunga was planning to go in this matter.

"I must say in all honesty and with all due respect to his

Eminence that it is hard to know how much he understands, how far he is prepared to go. Does he have the courage? It seems to me not. He appears timid. He is a holy man." Ndingi was to write in his diary.

In a way Ndingi felt, in spite of the cardinal's righteous indignation, that he had to fight the battle alone if necessary. If the cardinal joined in decisively, that would be good. If he held back, that would not deter him from going on. For him, he was fighting "the good fight" and he was pegging it on no other person other than himself and the cross of justice.

Seeing that politicians continued to incite the people and the clashes persisted, Ndingi upped the ante a little bit, this time throwing a more pointed challenge at the president. In a manner both daring and shocking, Ndingi asked the president if he was in the know about what was happening in his country. He did this in a statement issued from the Bishop's House in Nakuru on April 24, 1992 in which he claimed that what was happening was a futile attempt by KANU to resist the wind of change and that those in power were the ones masterminding the killings. Then he raised three questions:

> Can a government which is unwilling to take stern action for the security of its people now have any credibility for the future?
> Does the president not know what is happening? If not, why not? Where is his Massive intelligence network? Where are his Massive security forces? Why is there a bias towards one ethnic community in the implementation of security in these troubled areas?
> Why so soon after the president's call for peace at Turbo, should the murderous clashes resume in that area again? Would any credible government allow such things to happen? Is there a credible government at the moment?[1]

---

[1] Statement by Ndingi; *April 24, 1992*

Then he took the government by its horns: "If the present government cannot ensure the security and well being of its citizens, I strongly propose it resigns immediately and allows for fair and free elections in the hope that a future government will ensure peace and security for all Kenyans."

Was Ndingi a lone voice or was it a case of the madness of an entire nation disturbing a solitary mind? What had started as a low pitch call for sanity to prevail was finding resonance with many other church leaders and like-minded politicians in the country. By and by, the chorus for an end to the clashes started echoing in every part of the country. On 10th April 1992, the Kenya Episcopal Conference under the chairmanship of Archbishop Z. Okoth and the National Council of Churches of Kenya wrote a joint letter to the president asking to see him on the issue of the clashes. The letter was both a plea and an accusation.

"Whether you like it or not, the people have lost confidence in you and the people close to you," part of the letter said. "At present you seem to be securing the interests of a small clique of the rich and powerful who are surviving at the cost of blood and misery of thousands of small people."

Amidst all this, Ndingi's voice became the unmistakable cry of a man in a mono - maniacal search for justice. More and more statements continued to be churned out, the priests continued to gather information and to release updated statements on the situation; Ndingi was unrelenting in his support. He understood quite well that he was in the eye of the storm and that he most likely would not emerge unscathed. True to expectations, politicians started attacking him, some even waging personal attacks on him. Fortunately, his priests literally threw a cordon around him.

## A Voice Unstilled

In 1993, Ndingi issued a press statement to the effect that there were strange people operating in a house off Nakuru-Njoro road. There was a lot of activity at night in the farm, he said and people were afraid that they were planning attacks. The then Provincial Commissioner, Ishmael Chelang'a, refuted the allegations and said that the bishop must have gathered those rumours in a bar.

The priests in Nakuru were livid. Chelang'a had touched a landmine and the priests came down on him with the fury of injured buffaloes. They accused the PC of lack of respect for men of God and of imputing improper motives on the bishop, "Our bishop does not go to bars," they thundered. They also accused Chelang'a of lack of regard to God and of showing disrespect to the many Christians who had faith in their bishops.

Ndingi did not have to speak, "He was well protected by God and his people," says Fr Moses Muraya, the Vicar General of the Catholic Diocese of Nakuru. But the priests, in a biting sense of humour had a parting shot for Chelang'a: "If indeed the bishop got the rumours from a bar," they said, "then the people in the bar were more informed than the government."

The priests organised a demo against the PC immediately. Chelang'a realised that he could not beat the might of the Church, backed off, and apologised to Ndingi. All that while, Ndingi kept mum. His priests did the ranting.

The clergymen were assuming greater status in the fight for democracy and human rights. Ndingi's voice backed up by the entire assembly of bishops, both Catholic and Protestant continued to reverberate. Politicians began to feel uncomfortable and started to issue threats. But they were paid back, coin for coin by the bishop, the audacity of whom astounded them.

Ndingi's popularity among the people was rising almost

astronomically. One day in 1993, he was slated to visit Elburgon and celebrate Mass there but he was committed elsewhere and he therefore sent Fr Patrick Kanja to represent him. Fr Kanja recalls that when he arrived in Elburgon, seated in Ndingi's vehicle, the sight that met him astounded him. On every street, there were hordes of people from all denominations. He could tell this by the many *akorinos*, wearing their white turbans who were jumping up and down and singing songs of praise for the bishop. His popularity was not confined to just Catholics. His fame had spread far and wide and everyone, no matter their religion, embraced him.

Kanja did not know how to handle the situation. Here were thousands of people who had walked from every village in Elburgon expecting to see Bishop Ndingi but he was not there. Kanja felt very small sitting in Ndingi's car but he was touched by the overwhelming support the people showed. After the Mass, one man of the *Akorino* sect, the members of whom had sat through the Mass stood up and told the priest: "Go and thank Bishop Ndingi for what he has done for us. Tell him we are all very grateful and please tell him never to give up." Fr Kanja remembers that the man was quivering with emotion as he said this. He was referring to the fight the bishop had put up and to the material help he had given those afflicted by clashes. For he had mobilised pick-ups to take medicine, water and clothes to the victims in the absence of any government support.

### Like-minded allies

Ndingi found like-minded allies in the person of Maina Kiai, who was to become the chairman of the Kenya National Human Rights Commission at the turn of the decade and Prof. Wangari Maathai who was later to be awarded the Nobel Prize for her fight against social injustice. Maathai, the environmentalist-cum politician, was one of the most vocal politicians at the time and one who was constantly in the government's bad books. The government could not condone any occasion where Wangari was present or where she was addressing people. Her pairing up with Ndingi was particularly seen as hair-raising and the government constantly kept her in check.

On March 3, 1993 there was a meeting to discuss the rehabilitation of the displaced people at the hall of Christ the King Cathedral in Nakuru and Professor Maathai was invited. The embassies of Canada, Germany and Netherlands had also sent representatives to give views on how best to resettle the people. There were many people gathered at the gate of the Cathedral. As the bishop and the professor walked from the bishop's office to the cathedral, they were met by an astonishing sight. The cathedral had been cordoned off. There were General Service Unit (GSU) - a dreaded group of the administration police force - and Criminal Investigation Department (CID) personnel all around. The police were fully armed, "as if they were at war" and they were stopping people from entering the compound. Priests were required to identify themselves before they could be allowed entry into their church. Though they put up a strong resistance, the police were not in any mood to compromise. They stopped the meeting but the publicity it gained was more than enough to arouse the sensibilities of the nation as to what was going on in the Rift Valley.

Professor Maathai's crusade did not have the benefit of awe and fear as that of the bishop. She was a marked person in a way that the bishop was not. The bishop, however, lent her every kind of support. Her relentless battle with the government had started a little earlier when she mounted a serious campaign against the construction of Kenya Times Tower (KTT) in Uhuru Park. Wangari's view was that the construction of the complex would ruin the city and turn it into a concrete jungle. Almost single handedly, she waged a war against the development, drawing the international community to her cause and earning quite a number of enemies but also admirers. Members of the ruling party, KANU, were never comfortable with her. They railed, and threatened her so many times that she was in constant fear for her life; she was constantly in need of protection. Together with another crusader, Fr Ndikaru wa Teresia who had also waged an environmental crusade against a company called Kel Chemicals in Thika, were people on the run. Kel Chemicals was emitting harmful gases into the environment; endangering the lives of those living in the sorrounding.

In 1992, Wangari was at the peak of her crusade. This was also the time that her life was totally threatened. She was followed everywhere and was never sure of where she would be the following day. Where could she hide from the seeming omnipresence of security people? As they say, it is in the middle of danger that those who are threatened find the best refuge. Bishop Ndingi even though a marked man, arranged to house Wangari.

On March 2nd, 1993, he arranged with Fr Ndikaru wa Teresia[1] and Fr Francis Mirango to assist the professor go into hiding in Nakuru. This was a risky and almost impossible mission. Every one knew Wangari and the route to Nakuru was full of roadblocks. Besides, Fr Ndikaru himself was also a marked man. But this was a time to take risks and whichever way one looked at it, it was better to try out the mission than wait and get caught unawares.

[1] Editor of *Mwananchi Magazine*

Fr Ndikaru was to meet Wangari at Uthiru, ten kilometres from the city. The location was ideal because the place was teeming with people. No one seemed to notice a sickly looking lady, dejected to the core, wearing a *bui bui* and gazing into nothingness as if she had lost all hope of living. Those who saw her must have dismissed her as another Somali lady probably looking for her kin in the densely populated and cosmopolitan suburb.

Fr Ndikaru arrived at 9.35 a.m. The scrawny lady recognised the white Toyota Corolla car, registration KAA 203G and ambled towards it. She opened the door and got onto the back, slumping down like a patient collapsed. The car started off at a steady speed. No suspicions aroused, it got onto the highway and started the 140 kilometre journey to Nakuru.

At Kamandura-Limuru road, they came across the first road block. The car slowed down, the police peered in and saw a Somali lady. They waved the vehicle on. The next road-block was at Delamere in Naivasha. The police were not interested in a ragged looking man wearing a cap and a Somali lady seated at the back. They probably thought it was a taxi, so they waved it on.

But in Gilgil, tougher luck was awaiting them. The people manning the road-block were not regular police but GSU personnel. These would be more difficult to fool than the others. They waved down the vehicle. At this point the occupants of the vehicle said a prayer in Kikuyu , "*Mwathani utugitire na utuiguire tha*" (God protect us and have mercy on us)

"Where are you going?" a burly GSU man asked in a rude and abrasive voice, all the time training his eyes into the vehicle and the figure slumped at the back. Fr Ndikaru thought that the officer would recognise Wangari and his heart raced with terror. He was cold and full of fear. "I have never felt that kind of fear in my life," he was to later say. He was nearly responding when the officer cut in;

"*Kwani Mama ni Mgonjwa,*" (Is the old lady sick?)

"*Eee ni mgonjwa sana*" (yes, she is very sick). It was a holy lie and "God would forgive me," Fr Ndikaru recalled.

"*Haya basi kimbia haraka umpeleke hospitali pale Gilgil*" (then hurry and take her to hospital in Gilgil).

"That was the Holy Spirit at work," Fr Ndikaru told Maathai who also could not see it any other way.

They went past the other road blocks and up to the vicinity of the Bishop's house. Just ten metres from the house was another road-block manned by a handful of police officers in uniform and others in civilian clothes. Since there were no mobile phones at the time, there was no way of communicating that they were nearing the gate. The arrangements had been done two days earlier and according to the plan, they were to arrive at the residence at 1.10 pm. It was now 1.08 pm so Ndikaru knew they were fully expected. The officers looked at the car and the old lady and were not interested. At the residence, the gate was promptly opened by Mr Samson Mwangi, the bishop's driver, who pretended not to have a clue who the passengers were. But in fact, Mwangi knew what was going on. He had been expecting Maathai but feared that the police who were hovering around the residence would discover the plan and scuttle it. So a few minutes later, a group of nuns came passing by. Watched by the squadron of officers on either side of the road, Mwangi thought that his chance to distract them had come.

"How are you, Sisters?' Mwangi greeted them, loud enough for the officers to hear.

"We are well, how is the bishop?" they asked. They knew Mwangi quite well.

"The bishop is okay. But what are you doing here? You should be at the stadium where I hear Professor Wangari Maathai is addressing a mammoth crowd right now."

"Where?" the nuns asked in astonishment.

"I hear it is at the stadium, that is where I hear everyone is."

From the corner of his eye, Mwangi could see the exasperated countenance of the officers. They obviously believed they had been caught flat-footed. Some of them gathered themselves up hastily and left while others hurriedly worked their walkie talkies.

At that particular moment the white car with its surprising cargo drove up to the gate. The police at this point in time were not interested in who was inside since they already knew the whereabouts of their target.

Ndikaru dropped the professor, right in front of the police officers and after fifteen minutes started on his way back to Nairobi. At Gilgil again, he was stopped. The officers recognised him as the man with the sick lady. One of the officers approached him:

"*Eeh, habari tena?*" (How are you again?) he asked,

"*Umempeleka mama hospitali?*" (You have taken the lady to hospital?) and before Fr Ndikaru could answer, the GSU officer told him, "*Usijali mama atapona. Wanaume ni kujikaza*" (Don't worry, the lady will be well. Men should be brave and strong.)

Ndingi knew he was taking a risk of immeasurable proportions. But he believed that Wangari needed protection and that she was fighting for a just cause. He saw her as a comrade in the fight for social justice.

As his popularity rose, so did Ndingi's unpopularity among the ruling class. Annoyed at the outspokenness of the bishops, the Nakuru mayor then, Mr Korir, who was a brother to the

Eldoret Bishop Cornelius Korir suggested that all bishops should have their fingers chopped off. Ndingi promptly responded; "We will start with your brother." The politician was never to repeat that statement.

Bishop Korir had distinguished himself as a fighter for justice and he was at the forefront of helping the victims despite the fact that he belonged to a community that was identified with the ruling class then.

In 1993, as Father Francis Mirango was going to say Mass in the clash hit Molo, he was arrested, bundled into a police Land Rover and driven straight to the police station where charges of entering a restricted area were preferred against him. Being the procurator of the diocese, Father Mirango was therefore in a position to marshal the resources of the diocese to help victims of the clashes. He was also very close to Ndingi as they lived in the same house and he was as bold as the bishop in rising up against injustice. This did not endear him to the government.

The Church was vocal in defence of the priest, but the government alleged that Fr Mirango had no authority to say Mass in a restricted area and that not even his bishop had the authority to send him to say Mass in such an area. The case generated a lot of publicity with priests jamming the courtroom every day the case was mentioned, bedecked in their priestly robes. This somewhat scared the government. The case was giving it the kind of publicity it did not require at that time. In October 1994, the Attorney General withdrew the case.

As Ndingi continued to command huge hearing and attention and as he stepped up his fight with the government, the politicians saw a chink through which they could start piercing his credibility. And sure enough they found a way of going about it. Because most of the homeless were members of the Kikuyu community, the others running to their kin in the neighbouring districts, the Church was involved a great deal in tending to them.

Some politicians took advantage of this and created the impression that Ndingi was only helping members of one community. This was meant to germinate into a full scale revolt against the bishop. In fact, the then secretary to the Cabinet, Prof. Philip Mbithi issued a statement in October 1993 alleging that the Church had supported only one section of the communities affected by the clashes. But Ndingi was not to take this lying down. He wrote a scathing letter to Mbithi pointing out that his record and that of the Church in the clash-torn areas was well known by not just Catholics but also by the followers of other religions and even the local administration.

Mbithi accused Ndingi of telling lies about the situation in a report to the United Nations, Amnesty International and the British Refugee Council but Ndingi pointed out that whenever he spoke or acted, it was out of a clear understanding of the situation in his area. "If you contest what I am saying," he asked Mbithi, "are you prepared to swear on the Bible that what you have said is true and that what I say is false? I am willing to swear on the Bible that what I say is true."

The letter to Mbithi was a personal challenge to the head of the civil service to uphold integrity and truth, to be honest about what was happening and to sacrifice the need to serve his masters by falsehood at the altar of truth and justice:

> The time has come when we must all speak the truth for the sake of our people and not divide them further through falsehoods, even if we have to say what does not please our political masters. There is a Kamba proverb which says: *Utatavya ni mwana ndamui, na utatavya nithe ndamui* (There is a time when a

father must listen to his son as well as a son to his father). So I write you this letter, dear professor Mbithi, to remind you that as a Christian you will have to answer for the conduct of your high office before God, the God of truth, justice and love. God knows where the truth lies in Nakuru today. When we stand before him in judgment – as one day we most surely will – he will have only one of two words to say to us: come or go. You must decide whether you wish to serve truth or falsehood, peace and justice or hatred and the division of our country[3].

As Mbithi made his allegations other politicians continued to poison people's minds. Christians started echoing the same allegations and soon came to believe that the Church was indeed only assisting victims from one community. This gained currency in Kaplong and Kericho where it was openly said that the bishop was against the government and pro members of the Kikuyu community.

On June 5, 1992, Ndingi received a letter from a man calling himself "a Catholic faithful of our diocese and a resident of Sotik." The letter accused the bishop of a host of misdeeds, the most serious being what he called "the marginalisation of a section of our flock, the Kalenjins." The letter accused the bishop of only aiding the Kikuyu victims.

> You, our bishop, transported, fed, clothed, provided medical attention to and consoled the Kikuyu victims of the clashes. There was nothing wrong with [sic] doing this. What makes our hearts bleed is that you totally neglected the Kipsigis and other Kalenjin victims who had to trek through wild-infested forests to languish in unsheltered camps with no food, medical care, spiritual care and consolation.

The seven-page hand-written letter stated that the Kalenjins

---

[3]letter to Mbithi, October 15, 1993

would not be making offerings in the Church and they had rather belong to the wider archdiocese where they would feel more at home.

A little earlier, on May 27, 1992 a group of people from the Kalenjin community had called a press conference and echoed the same sentiments. The story was published in *Kenya Times* on May 28 and it was followed by a scathing editorial which alleged that the bishop was a supporter of Mwai Kibaki's Democratic Party. It was not lost on Ndingi that the letter from the parishioner was dated May 26, 1992 (though received on June 5, 1992) just a day before the press conference and the editorial in the KANU-owned newspaper, a pointer to a well-orchestrated campaign to discredit the bishop.

On 3rd August 1992, Ndingi replied to the letter, apologising for not writing earlier and attempting to correct the parishioner:

> I have been to Bomet, Segemet, Marinyin, Litein and Ndanai. The impression I got after talking to people does not support your allegation. On Saturday August, 22, at 10 a.m I shall be in Kaplong to meet the people. May I extend you an invitation to attend and hear what they have against me or for me. Please come. If you are not able to attend on 22nd, may I have your telephone number and I will make arrangements to meet you in Nairobi for a frank discussion.

The bishop also said in the letter that at no time did he accuse the Kalenjin of being behind the crimes in the area. "Like any other group in the diocese, they are my people."

The bishop's letter was a humble response concluding with the words, "Please do all you can so that we can meet on Saturday August 22, 1992 at Kaplong or advise me on where and when we can meet in Nairobi. I sincerely thank you for your prayers and assure you of my own."

Ndingi knew the meeting at Kaplong which is populated by members of the Kipsigis community, would be charged. But he was willing to plunge into it and defuse the tension that was building against the diocesan leadership. Attacks between the Kikuyu and Kalenjin had reached alarming levels, with the latter attacking the Kikuyus who would seek refuge in schools. When Ndingi heard of the incidents he visited the schools and gathered the displaced to some centres where they would get some help. When the Kipsigis were attacked by Kikuyus, they would also run away, but to their kin and kith around the same place. So it was less obvious that they required as much help as the Kikuyus did. The fact that those who got the bulk of the help were Kikuyus was misinterpreted to mean that Ndingi was partial. It was this complaint that made him call a meeting in Kaplong, Litein and Bomet.

In all cases, he sat through the meetings and listened to all manner of accusations. Some people insulted him to his face but he did not raise his voice or lose his temper. Fr Patrick Kanja who was there at the meetings and who interpreted for the bishop (he understands and speaks Kipsigis) remembers the kind of insults and accusations the bishop had to withstand. At times, he feared that the crowd would become violent and stone them. When he looked at Ndingi, he remembers, the bishop was a picture of serenity. He hardly portrayed any fear or lack of confidence.

At one point, one man rose up and accused the bishop of concentrating on development projects in Kikuyu dominated areas. The bishop listened and asked the man calmly: "How many of those projects are in Kikuyu areas and how many are in the Kipsigis areas?" The man did not know. The bishop who had all the facts at his finger tips proceeded to enumerate how many projects there were and where each was. He pointed out that while Nakuru, which was seen as a Kikuyu dominated area did not have a church-initiated hospital, there was one in Ravine, which was in Baringo district and another in Kaplong, Kericho district. He also pointed out that the Church had built a number of dispensaries in places like Loret and Kipchimchim. He allowed everyone who had a grievance to vent it out and he responded to each of them calmly. This was quite uncharacteristic of the bishop because he was given to quick temper and momentary anger. But at the end of the meetings, the people had understood the bishop better and some were heard muttering, much later, "The bishop is right."

This was great relief for the priests who admired his leadership. But there was something that always unnerved them – his bravery. Some priests thought that Ndingi was pushing matters too far and feared that a cornered government could turn around and harm him. Memories of Alexander Muge, the Anglican bishop who died in a suspicious road accident in 1990, were too fresh in their minds. Many believed that Muge was killed because of his unflattering attitude to government. A few days before his death, Muge had been warned by a cabinet minister, Peter Okondo, that he could lose his life if he continued criticising the government.

Okondo said, "If he and Bishop, Dr Henry Okullu, visit Busia district, they will not come back alive because they want to poison the minds of Busia people against the government. They hardly appreciate anything KANU does to try and uplift the living standards of the people."

Twenty-four hours before he died, Muge had declared that his life was in danger. But as if in defiance of those threats,

## In the eye of the storm

Muge proceeded with a trio to Busia on August 14th, just two days after the warning. It was difficult then for many people to accept that Muge's death was a result of a normal accident. If it were true that the government had a hand in the death of Muge, many wondered, what would prevent it from silencing the voice of Ndingi, the one man that the whole country had come to know because of his unrelenting fight for justice?

Father Kanja remembers how concerned the other priests were about Ndingi's safety, "Often, we feared for his security and we made it our business to always know where and how he was."

At one time, his house was bugged and some strange vehicles would follow him. He knew all this but he neither expressed fear nor tried to hide. As if to warn him that the worst was to follow, his house was burgled. The burglars seemed to have secured a key from, the bishop believes, some former member of staff who had been sacked. The thieves stole some rings, a crucifix and small articles—the bishop's symbols of authority. To make it look like they had broken into the house through the window, they shattered one of the window panes and left it open. This was just a warning that whoever those people were, they could get him whenever they wanted.

The priests were convinced that that was no simple burglary. It was meant to intimidate the bishop. The priests' main concern was that the bishop resolved to carry on even when all guns and bombs were exploding around him. He was not afraid; even afraid to die. His motto was that no one died from 'morning to evening [sic].' "If I have to die," a priest remembers Ndingi as saying, "I will die because of the truth not because of any wrong doing."

Ndingi believed that a religious leader worth his salt had to obey his conscience and keep the faith even when death lurked in the bushes around him:

> Conscience is the most secret core and sanctuary of man. There he is alone with God whose voice echoes in his depths... faith or belief demands the fullness of conscience. In faith, a man accepts gratefully the self-manifestation of God and opens his deepest nature of God ...[4]

Much as this caused concern to the priests, it was also a morale booster for them. They too could speak out fearlessly; and they did. If they were seen as storm petrels by those who believed in the system, those in pursuit of justice and human rights viewed them as messiahs in a stormy age.

Realising that the crusade Ndingi had started was beginning to capture the attention of the international community, the government started to change the tone and redirect their accusations elsewhere. They would begin to blame the victims of the clashes. They accused them of being squatters in other people's pieces of land and of taking oaths to "continue perpetrating the atrocity." The opposition, whose members, ironically, were the most afflicted ones, were accused of engineering the clashes. Blaming the victim in a senseless war like the one taking place in the Rift Valley, was a major temptation of warlords. In a letter, Mbithi had alleged that there was oathing taking on a Massive scale in the Rift Valley and accused Ndingi of not speaking about it. Ndingi took him on, asking him pertinent questions about what was happening;

> As you well know, I have always spoken out against oathing as an evil practice and I have declared that, to embrace an evil like this is no way to right perpetrated wrongs. Why have a

---

[4] Address to University of Nairobi students, August 29, 1987.

people under attack resorted to oathing at this time? Is it not that, frightened and defenseless as they are, they resort to this primitive practice because they find themselves with their backs to the wall, without redress of any kind, and are driven by fear and desperation? There can be no peace until the people feel secure and know that they will be defended by the forces of law and order. There can be no peace without justice.[5]

In some ways, Ndingi managed to steady the trajectory of his crusade. There was little humanitarian assistance getting to the victims and there were no government officials interested in visiting them. Everything was left to the Church.

Ndingi's crusade against social injustice and violation of human rights could be seen in two ways: first, as a man of God and second as a citizen of the country. In most of the letters he addressed to the authorities, he described himself as a citizen and bishop of the Catholic Diocese of Nakuru. This gave him immeasurable weight to deal with the monstrosities confronting the country.

Writing about Ireland and the problems it was encountering at the turn of the last century, the Irish author, James Joyce quite seminally captured the impulse that drives a man to fight against injustice in *A Portrait of the Artist*: "When the soul of a man is born in this country there are nets flung at it to hold it back from flight."

Ndingi was firmly in those nets and he was flying by them. As a citizen of the country, his soul was in the nation and he was concerned about what was happening to his beloved country and her people. As a man of God, he was concerned at the symmetry of evil enacting itself and draining out the truth of God from the bowels of the nation. He was concerned about the moral

---

[5] Letter to Mbithi.

impunity with which those who executed ethnic hatred had operated and the disgusting silence on the part of those who could have brought the skirmishes to an end.

He was also concerned that the politicians were bringing in the worst in men, replicating evil in their hearts and he refused to ascribe to Everyman's view that evil is the nature of mankind. Still he refused to accept that politics, as one theorist put it, has always been the systematic organisation of hatreds. He was convinced that the evil he was experiencing could be fought and that it only needed a few brave Kenyans to do it.

The bishop due to his gallant fight for justice attained a larger-than-life status in the country. He was not just a Catholic cleric but some would see him as a political figure set to redeem the people from the political ills dogging the country.

When the opposition was trying to coalesce and come up with a formula to beat Moi in the 1997 elections, there was a great deal of debate as to who their candidate should be. There was Mwai Kibaki of the Democratic Party, Kijana Wamalwa of Ford-Kenya, and Raila Odinga of the National Democratic Party on one side of the spectrum. Kenneth Matiba of Ford Asili and Martin Shikuku were also strong contenders. In 1992, the opposition had fielded six – Kibaki, Jaramogi, Matiba, Anyona, Mwau and Ng'ang'a – and all had failed to trounce Moi then. It was now becoming increasingly clear that the opposition was headed for another slaughter and the debate continued. They needed a person who had a national outlook and one who would be capable of trouncing Moi. Who should be their candidate? The name that was coming to mind was that of Ndingi. Indeed, the Langata MP and one of the front runners for the seat then, Raila Odinga had earlier told a meeting of opposition MPs in Embu town that opposition parties would choose a clergyman as a compromise candidate to run against Moi in 1997. Whispers started doing the rounds that the bishop was being fronted as a joint opposition candidate for the presidency and some of the opposition politicians started forming caucuses to popularise the idea. The concept was that because none of the opposition leaders was willing to step down, the search for a compromise candidate should be extended beyond the political landscape. It should probably consider a clergyman with strong credentials and one who was involved in agitating for human rights.

Bishop Ndingi's name kept coming up. Opposition politicians thought that a Catholic bishop was an exciting prospect because they thought, he would take advantage of the numerical strength of the Church throughout the country. Nzeki was also being touted because he was thought to be more acceptable to a cross-section of opposition leaders and due to the fact that a number of opposition leaders, Kibaki and Shikuku being some of them, were also Catholic.

For a time, some sections of the country viewed Ndingi not just as a Catholic bishop but a future president, a compromise candidate who might just manage to topple Moi from power. "Ndingi for President," was a phrase already forming in people's minds. In fact, some politicians started seeing the bishop as the right material for a care-taker president, an acknowledgement that Moi's formidability made it virtually impossible for the present crop of politicians to remove him. They needed someone out of the political fold, one who was popular enough to reach out to all corners of the country.

In November 1995, hopes for a Catholic bishop presidency were cruelly dashed. Ndingi came out to clarify that he had no such ambitions and that he was comfortable remaining a priest, "My ambition in life is to be a good, simple priest." The rumours that he would be a candidate were by now so widespread that some people came to believe them to be true. As he made the announcement Ndingi also disclosed that two cabinet ministers had approached him wanting to know if it was true that he had been offered the prospect by the opposition. His answer was an emphatic no. He had not been approached by the opposition and if he was, the answer would still be no.

Though this dampened the hearts of those who thought that a Ndingi candidacy would be the best way out, it gladdened the hearts of many that the bishop still remained a crusader for social justice and human rights and probably would remain so for a long time.

During the debate for constitutional reforms, Ndingi adopted the same position he had during the queue voting and the clashes. He wanted the constitution not only reviewed but the people to also be given a bigger say in the reforms.

People continued to die, the government continued to play possum, politicos continued to hound him, but they never quite understood the enigma that was Raphael Ndingi Mwana 'a Nzeki. At no time was he to give up.

# CHAPTER TWELVE

## *Oh, another Pope is here*

Every five years, bishops all over the world are supposed to make what is called the quinquennial *ad limina* visit to Rome. According to ancient custom and Church Law, every bishop who heads a diocese must go to Rome to make a pilgrimage known as *ad limina apostolorum*: "to the thresholds of the apostles"

The bishops normally make the quinquennial visit in national groups or regional groups to simplify scheduling and allow more concentrated discussions of local problems. George Wiegel, a Vatican expert and biographer of the late John Paul II observed that during the pontificate of Paul VI, a bishop's *ad limina* visit involved a brief personal meeting with the Pope and a series of meetings with curial officials. But John Paul changed the standard *ad limina* programme to give himself more time to interact with bishops, individually and as regional or national groups.

John Paul II continued with that tradition in which every *ad limina* included a personal, one-on-one meeting with each bishop. The sessions lasted from fifteen minutes to half-hour or more. This was a private encounter. Under John Paul II, no translators were allowed into the meeting room and the discussions mainly centered on the operations of individual dioceses and the situation in the bishops' home countries. This presented a good opportunity for the bishops to know the Pope better and tell him precisely what was on their minds.

It is also the Pope's way of getting to know the world's episcopate and, in the case of John Paul II the visits, as Wiegel observed, were also another of his teaching instruments of the papacy and occasions for him to offer an insight into what the Pope thought about the situation of particular local churches.

During one of those *ad limina* visits in 1976 during Paul VI's reign, the bishops from Kenya filed into the Vatican where they were to meet the Pope. It was a tradition for bishops to wear their bishopric attire of black soutanes. The white soutane is usually a preserve of the Pope. But on this day, Bishop Ndingi stood out distinctively among the Kenyan bishops. He was wearing a white soutane. The cardinal in charge of protocol had tried in vain to have him remove it and wear black like other bishops.

"No, this place is too hot for a black soutane," he replied, "I'm going to wear this one." The official politely tried to explain that only the Pope should wear that in the Vatican but Ndingi would hear none of it. The officials gave up. As the Pope greeted each one of the bishops, on that 26th day of November 1976, he came to where Ndingi was. As he proffered his hand, the Pope remarked cheekily, "Oh, and there is another Pope here." There was laughter and the matter ended there.

Later the Pope granted Ndingi a private audience for twenty-five minutes during which Ndingi handed him a personal letter. The Vatican officials wondered what Ndingi was telling the Pope but Ndingi had only raised concerns with the Pope about what was happening in his diocese. The letter outlined some concerns about the Church in Kenya, issues that were quite close to Ndingi's heart and which involved training of priests. He was particularly concerned about what he called a move to ask or force the missionary bishops to send their students of philosophy to Rome. "I feel strongly that this would be a move towards the wrong direction. Our preference would be to educate our own students for the priesthood and ordination at home. After ordination and a few years of pastoral experience and maturity, only then would the local ordinary be able to judge which of his priests was ready and well prepared to face the pressures and the forces of the modern world outside of his own milieu. It is only after this that a young priest is judged suitable or unsuitable for studies overseas."

What Ndingi was asking for was a greater say for the bishops and closer scrutiny of seminarians back home before they could be ordained. This was to be a pet topic for Ndingi who kept emphasising on proper sifting of seminarians before they could be ordained. But more important was the audacity of the bishop to speak his mind when all others were reluctant or feared doing so.

Quite out of character, Ndingi never asked for any financial assistance for his diocese when bishops met the Pope. The Pope must have wondered why. So after the audience, he sent an aide, Fr John Magee to ask if the bishop had wanted any money.

'No," replied the bishop, "I came for *ad limina* not on a begging mission," he told Fr Magee. Magee insisted that the bishop needed some money and had asked the Pope for some. Ndingi stuck to his guns, "I did not ask for any money."

Nevertheless, the Pope offered him $10,000. The bishop thought it rude to decline and took it. He later donated it to the Bahati Novitiate for the completion of their building.

If the Vatican officials were uneasy with Ndingi's easy and audacious manner, they never showed it. But he records that when, during the same occasion, he visited the Propaganda Fide offices (The Congregation for the Evangelisation of Peoples) the reception was 'rather cool and subdued.' He never got to know why but it was easy to guess.

The case of the white soutane was not just an isolated incident of a man trying to beat the weather. In many cases, it eloquently told a story of the peculiarities of the man known as Bishop Raphael Ndingi Mwana 'a Nzeki. In fact, there are many other photographs extant of the Pope and Bishop Ndingi in white soutanes. As Fr Dennis Newman, the former administrator of the Catholic Diocese of Nakuru and the one Ndingi took over from as the head of the diocese was to remark, "the more distinguished cardinals, patriarchs and archbishops donned the black!"

Right from his names, which excluded his first one (Raphael), Ndingi was a man who, as Bishop John Njenga acknowledges, liked to do things differently. Was he an iconoclast or just a man who loved to be different, one who liked following his spirit?

Those who know him wonder why, instead of the normal bishop's hat, Ndingi wears a different four-cornered one. This is the kind of bishopric article you would rarely see on any other bishop's head. But Ndingi has always worn it. He treasures it. He says it was a gift from Ethiopia. Though he will not discuss it, even for the purposes of this book, some priests confided in the writers that the hat is symbolic to the bishop in a deep way. It signifies his love of Africa and he feels that the hat is a celebration of the inclusion of that which is good in Africa into the integument of the Church of Rome.

As far as the history of the Catholic Church in Kenya goes, there has always been a standard way of ordaining priests. They go to the junior seminary and then proceed to the senior seminary on a programme that runs for seven years. After that, one could be ordained deacon then priest.

But Ndingi once broke this tradition. He ordained a catechist priest. The story of Fr Joseph M'Lengera is told with awe in Nakuru and represents the most incontrovertible evidence yet that when Ndingi believed in the goodness of a cause, he never looked back no matter what the norms decreed.

M'Lengera was one the most devout catechists in the diocese of Nakuru. In fact he attended Ndingi's consecration in Kampala in 1969. When he returned home, he kept reading of the bishop in Machakos in *The Catholic Mirror* to feed his curiousity on Ndingi. Ndingi's transfer to Nakuru marked a turning point in this catechist's life. On November 8, 1970 during the ordination of Fr Peter Kairo, who later became the bishop of Nakuru and now the Archbishop of Nyeri, M'Lengera met Ndingi face to face. It was the first time the two were meeting. After that they were to meet more regularly as they both worked in Nakuru district. During the course of their interaction, Ndingi came to admire the catechist's devotion and diligence.

One day in 1976, M'Lengera received a visitor in his house. It was a priest sent by the bishop to ask one question; "Are you interested in becoming a priest?" The question was contained in a letter addressed to him.

M'Lengera was lost for words. He knew that there were rigorous procedures involved in the ordination of priests. One had to study at a seminary and attain a certain level of education. But M'Lengera was a simple person from Tigania, Meru district who had one day, drifted to Rift Valley and settled in Nakuru in the early years of the Emergency. There was no primary school where he was born and he therefore had no benefit of early education. He secured work as a casual labourer on a dairy farm run by European settlers in Elementaita. He was not a Christian then, but there was a certain spirit burning in him. So he used his first wages to buy a Bible which he received by post from the CMS bookshop at a cost of three shillings.

He did not know how to read or write as there was no school in Elementaita and it was only through sheer effort that he learned a bit of reading and writing. Much later, he secured a job at a saw mill on the edge of Mau Forest, near Njoro. Here, he came face to face with the Catholic Church in the name of Fr Gerry McCluskey. He started attending Mass and helping in the Church. In 1955, he was baptised by Fr McCluskey. In 1956, he started working as a catechist after work and on Sundays. Another priest, Fr Tony Prunty bought him his first bicycle to enable him get around more easily to the other catechumenates. But his catechetical work was to prove his undoing. He lost his job in October 1957 because his catechetical work did not have the approval of the European settlers: his employers.

But another priest, Fr Brian Cunningham came to his rescue and employed him as a full-time catechist. By this time, he was in his late 20s and had never thought of marriage, believing that he was called to a more peculiar relationship with Christ. In 1961, he got an opportunity to join the Brothers of St Joseph Institution in Nyeri, where his stint did not last. He could not fit in and he went back to Elburgon. Still undaunted, he tried to join another congregation of Brothers in Kakamega, believing that to become a brother would be his best option in his life as a clergyman. But he failed after only one year and gave up. He settled down to becoming a catechist and consoled himself that if he could not reach the sun he could at least climb a plateau bathed by the sun's rays.

In May 1975, in recognition of his work, he was chosen to

go to Rome for the Holy Year commemoration to represent the catechists of Kenya.

So when the bishop popped the question, M'Lengera at first was incredulous. Was the bishop serious? But the priest emissary made it clear that the bishop required an answer, underlining the fact that he was serious.

"Has the bishop asked any other catechist this question?" he asked the priest.

"No" came the answer.

Why him? M'Lengera wondered. Of all the other catechists, why him? Perhaps it was God speaking through the bishop, M'Lengera concluded. He, nevertheless, took his time. A few days later he wrote back to the bishop accepting the offer.

It took almost two years for the bishop to get back to him on this matter. M'Lengera kept wondering whether the bishop had been serious with his request. Then one day, the bishop sent for M'Lengera and told him to get ready.

"The road to your priesthood has begun," he told him.

He was sent to West Pokot to study under the guidance of Fr Michael Dillon at Chepararia Parish. Fr Dillon was not a stranger to M'Lengera both having made acquaintance in Nakuru. After two years, he was sent to the Consolata Seminary where he attended classes and conferences for a year. In June 1980, he was sent to Bahati Parish in Nakuru to live with Fr Prunty and Fr Newman who again taught him the basics of priesthood. During the holidays, he stayed with Bishop Ndingi and on July 4, 1981, Joseph M'Lengera was ordained a priest in a precedent-setting ordination.

Why did Ndingi break the tradition to ordain a catechist as a priest? The answer is to be found in the man's character. When he believes in something or someone, he defends them to the last minute. Today Fr M'Lengera is a respected priest in the Catholic Diocese of Nakuru ministering to the sick and excelling in this area in a remarkable way. In many ways, his performance has vindicated Ndingi.

## The bishop's toothache

A fiercely disciplined man, Ndingi always kept a full diary, worked six days a week, only taking Wednesdays off. "He was a slave to a diary, which was always full," remarks Fr Newman, "it was indeed remarkable that he bound himself to the work in such an admirable, unselfish and disciplined way. He was exemplary in his life-style, simple, undemanding, a true follower of the Franciscan way."

That diary documents his day to day operations in a precise fashion. He would list down who he met on any given day, what they talked about and also put down his private feelings on matters preoccupying him that day.

"It was amazing to see that kind of order," Fr Newman says, "Order was and I still believe is, the bishop's middle name."

His orderly life was sometimes a nuisance to those who abhorred order. He knew where everything was in the house and he always kept everything in its place. He never expected a visitor to tamper with that order. If you wanted peace, you were advised to leave everything as you found it in the house.

Fr Francis Mirango who lived with him in the same house for five years was always amazed at the bishop's sense of order. "If he sent you to his bedroom to get something, he would tell you precisely where to find it," he says, "And it always was there."

His day started at 5.30 a.m. He would go to the chapel for prayers and meditations then go for Mass. At 6.30 a.m he would

## Oh, another Pope is here

have completed these chores after which he would listen to a BBC programme till 6.45 a.m. After this, he would sit down at 7.00 a.m for a light breakfast of fruits, toast and coffee with honey and never sugar as he read the morning papers. He would be in his office at 7.30 a.m, way before anyone else. At 1.00 p.m he would break for lunch and then take a short siesta between 2.15 p.m and 2.30 p.m. He would be in his office till 5.30 p.m.

At 6.00 p.m he would take walks in his compound saying his rosary. The rosary is something he never forgot to say and he would be at it for an hour until 7.00 p.m when he would take his supper. After that he would be back in his chapel for evening and night prayers.

Before he went to bed at 10.00 p.m he took his cup of Ovaltine. This he did without fail and it was his signal that he was ready to go to bed. This is a ritual that he observes till today.

An ardent swimmer,[1] Ndingi has always made it a point to tend to the body after tending to the soul. One priest remembers a day when, while swimming at the St Mary's school, Nairobi, he saw an old man swimming in the pool looking rather relaxed and in harmony with water. The priest plunged into the pool ready to race with the unstoppable old man. "How many hours do you spend in water?" he heard the familiar unmistakable voice. It was the bishop. The old man he had seen swim so ardently was his bishop.

"I only do 15 rounds," the priest answered. He was talking about full laps in an olympic-size swimming pool.

"Fifteen rounds?" exclaimed the bishop, "Are you serious? I wish I was younger. I used to do far more than that."

The priest and the bishop spent another hour or two just chatting. It is characteristic of Ndingi to fit in any conversation

---

[1] Up to this day, Ndingi still swims every Wednesday at 6 a.m

with anyone. He mixes freely with people, he easily strikes up a conversation and he is at home in every situation.

In Nakuru, the priests simply loved him. They remember that when bishops visited the seminary, it was only Ndingi who would gather up seminarians from his diocese and have them sit in a circle while he sat in the middle. He would bond with them and share freely.

"Work hard and pray," he would always exhort them. As a result, many seminarians from Nakuru Diocese were more confident, and in the words of Fr Muraya, proud to belong here.

Much as he was seen as an easy, humble man, Ndingi's temper could sometimes be explosive. When he was tired, he would lose his temper quite easily and when that happened, no one wanted to be near him. The priests had their way of assessing his mood. "How is he today?" they would ask and depending on the mood the bishop was in, the answer would come back, "he has a toothache. Stay away."

A toothache was the description they gave for the bishop's bad mood. However, his temper was not wholly implacable although it sometimes proved difficult to get through to him. Those who knew him nevertheless, were aware that this anger which was like the ebullition of boiling milk just needed a drop of cold water to calm it down.

Fr Kanja remembers a time when he hosted some visitors from abroad and needed to drive them to Nakuru town. His car had a faulty handbrake and he could not get the required spare part anywhere in town. He went to Ndingi to borrow his car, another indication of the man's simplicity; he could share his vehicle freely with his priests. Kanja explained that the handbrake was faulty and he parked it in the bishop's compound. He would be away for two days.

Upon return, he found a livid Ndingi who tore into him right in front of the visitors;

"How could you have been driving such a car?" he asked him, "How can you drive a car without a handbrake?"

Even before the priest could explain that he had already alerted him that the car was faulty, Ndingi pummeled him accusing him of carelessness and other unflattering deeds. The visitors were perplexed and they could see that the bishop was clearly upset. Kanja was embarrassed for having to endure such humiliation in front of foreign guests. Later, some tried to console Kanja and urged him to use the opportunity to get the bishop to buy him a new vehicle.

That very evening, Kanja felt he had to let the bishop know that it was wrong to embarrass him in front of visitors. He found Ndingi alone.

"Your Grace," he started, "I know it's your duty to correct me and I don't mind being corrected," Ndingi listened, "but next time you want to correct me, please don't do it in front of visitors. Just call me aside. Your Grace, you embarrassed me."

Kanja expected the bishop to erupt again. But Ndingi gave him a concerned, almost pious look. 'I am so sorry Father," he said, "I sincerely apologise."

Kanja was taken aback. He never expected such humility from his bishop.

"At that point," he says, "all I could do was to go home."

A stickler for honesty, Ndingi is famed for his intolerance of dishonesty. However grave your offence could be, there was a huge possibility of being forgiven if you told him the truth. Most priests who passed through his hands recall that if you did something wrong in the seminary that required the intervention of the bishop, Ndingi was sure to guide you and possibly save you if you told him the truth.

The case of a young seminarian attests to that. This young man would go on a drinking spree and get totally intoxicated. At some point Ndingi called him and asked him about the stories doing the rounds about his drinking habit. The seminarian gave Ndingi a long story about his innocence, but when the bishop got confirmation from another source that the seminarian used to actually get drank, he got wild. He berated the guy into submission, then sent him away without pronouncing a definite sentence on his fate. For if there is one thing that Ndingi is said to have agonised about, it was sending people away from the seminary. Even when the seminary recommended suspension, he would differ with the decision and recommend that the case be reviewed. This is how the seminarian escaped but he never dared utter a falsehood to the bishop again.

The seminarians of Nakuru Diocese always nestled in the feeling and hope that their bishop would give them a hearing no matter how grave their cases were. The seminary authorities were usually not happy with this lenient standard and if it turned out that the bishop was wrong on a particular case, they were heard to gleefully say, "We told him."

But this never detracted Ndingi from the path of mercy. He believed in giving people the benefit of doubt. If he got a wanting report about a priest, he would call them and discuss the issue at hand. If the priest convinced the bishop that he was not on the wrong, the bishop would be on his side and he would also defend him.

"It is important to trust people, sometimes to the extent of allowing them to make mistakes but not blunders," he once told a congregation of priests.

But those who have been unfortunate to encounter the bishop's rough side have lived to tell the tale. One case regularly cited was of a seminarian, who must have taken Ndingi's leniency for granted. After going through the training and as he was just about to be ordained deacon, Ndingi refused to ordain him with no explanation whatsoever. This rattled all the seminarians who all along had believed that their bishop was not capable of taking such harsh action.

In much the same way, Ndingi agonised for days over suspending errant priests, he would spend days trying to counsel the errant ones and would especially go out of his way to rescue them from their problems. But for one to benefit from the bishop's munificence, one had to be completely honest.

He once sent a missionary packing after a case of disobedience and defiance. This was at a time when the missionaries held sway in Nakuru Diocese and some expected to be treated preferentially. Ndingi did not fear anyone and he treated all, missionaries and the local clergy in the same way. In this particular incident, Ndingi sent his financial administrator, Fr Francis Mirango to Fr John O'Brien who was then in charge of the Longonot Parish to ensure that a borehole was drilled in the area. Fr O'Brien was one of those missionaries who had seemingly never accepted that the Church in the Diocese of Nakuru was Africanizing and that there was an African bishop in charge. Some priests described him as arrogant and uncooperative. Others thought that he was disdainful of black priests. Relations between O'Brien and Ndingi were at best dicey. When Ndingi sent Fr Mirango, Fr O'Brien even with the full knowledge that Mirango was the bishop's emissary did not allow the drilling of the borehole to commence.

"The bishop should have consulted me," he complained.

"That is why he sent me" Mirango retorted, "besides, the drilling of the borehole will be fully financed." The drilling was being financed by a German church organisation called Missio which was involved in uplifting the lives of communities in the Rift Valley and with whom the diocese had good relations. Sadly, Fr O'Brien could hear none of that.

Fr Mirango went back to the diocese and wrote a letter explaining that it was the wish of the diocese and the bishop to have a borehole drilled in Longonot to help the locals meet their water needs. Fr O'Brien, in what was tantamount to cocking a snook at the financial administrator, took the same letter and wrote on it in red, "for your safe keeping." Then he posted it back to the priest.

The bishop was out of the country at that time and Mirango waited for him to come back. Seething with anger and knowing that O'Brien had a habit of humiliating many including the bishop, Fr Mirango went straight to Ndingi and explained the unfolding events.

"Your grace," he told him, "I cannot take this attitude even though the priest is known for his condescending attitude to Africans."

Ndingi wrote to the priest asking him to explain. Fr O'Brien fulminated that it was wrong for the financial administrator to start developments in his parish without consulting him. Then he gave conditions: "It is either Fr Mirango is removed from the diocese as financial administrator and made to apologise to me, or I leave."

Ndingi was resolute. "You are the one to go," he told Fr O'Brien. He dispatched a priest that day, to ensure that the missionary packed his belongings and left the diocese. This sent a shiver in the world of the missionaries in Nakuru and also the local clergy. Fr O'Brien left the diocese and went to South Africa where, again, he could not cope and had to leave.

Much as Ndingi enjoyed good relations with missionaries there were some who were openly hostile to him and the other African priests. One, Fr Bobby Kavanagh, who was an inveterate loner and lived alone in his mission, could not allow another priest to hold brief when he was on leave. This led to the closure of the mission. Fr Kavanagh was deported in 1992 at the height of the clashes.

Ndingi's stand on specific matters of the Church did not go down very well with some priests. But he believed firmly that "the bishop is the one primarily responsible for evangelisation and for the ministry to the diocesan community."[2] His was to exercise leadership and authority. Authority did not mean shying away from taking hard decisions. Leadership did not mean pleasing everyone. "Authority without leadership results in one or other form of dictatorship, while leadership without authority creates chaos. Authority and leadership should supplement and complement each other."

Dialogue and consultation formed an important part of Ndingi's management style. He listened to all sides, as in the case with the Kaplong, Bomet and Litein incidents.

Dialogue, he believed, required a listening attitude and disposition to see the other person's point even if it was not acceptable to us. This was usually misconstrued as a weakness on the part of the bishop. But he had a theological explanation to the meaning of dialogue. He once told AMECEA bishops:

> Man as he is here and now, and as he would like to be, is both

---

[2] Address to AMECEA Pastoral Institute Gaba, 10th September 1990.

the subject and the object of every form of dialogue. We must try to get to know the other not just as he is, but also as he would like to be. A human being can only be at peace only when he has made a positive contribution to the decisions that affect his life. If his voice has been heard, even an unfavourable decision is tolerable. The heart finds peace when its convictions are listened to with openness and respect."[3]

His relationship with the lay people, priests and missionaries in Nakuru was based on this. This maxim, though, was not absolute. Ndingi is a mix of liberalism and conservatism. He may allow liberal opinions but he never would compromise on doctrinal matters. He would forgive moral failure but he would not forgive doctrinal failures. A priest going against the teachings of the Church or its doctrine immediately found an adversary in Ndingi. "Our vocation is to spread the saving message of Christ," he told Seminarians at St Augustine's Senior Seminary in Mabanga on October 25 1998, "To do this faithfully, we must spread the gospel *secundum mentem ecclesiae* (according to the mind of the Church). This was a term he would use much more regularly while addressing priests and seminarians for he believed that the Church's teachings must be adhered to no matter one's personal beliefs.

He also required, in full measure, commitment from the priests. The sincerely committed African priest, he believed and still does, is the best advertisement of priestly life amongst his people.

It was known among the clergy that Ndingi could walk with a priest when he was in trouble in a most fatherly way. He was

---

[3] Ibid

particularly vocal that the Church should not lose the services of a priest just because he could not be salvaged from the ways that were making such a priest depart from his vocation. But he also reprimanded in a fatherly way. However, all this was dependent on how honest one was with him." If he trusts you," says Fr Muraya, the Vicar General of Nakuru Diocese, "he can give you anything, defend you and die with you. His trust and generosity go overboard."

The priests also knew that when he was happy, he could give his all. When he was unhappy, he could give one hell.

Ndingi's generosity, is legendary. In Nakuru he loved a simple life, drove a simple car and gave to the Church almost all the gifts he got. And he expected the priests to give to the Church too. A priest who one day received, through the bishop, a gift of twenty thousand Kenya shillings in the 90s, got a rude shock when the bishop refused to hand it to him. He instead sent it to the priest's parish to be used as part of the Church finances.

One thing he never condoned was night driving especially by his priests. His house was always open to a late-travelling priest coming from a far-away parish. But there was a rider; do not come after eight. He did not expect to receive any visitor after eight in the evening and he did not expect a priest to be travelling after eight.

His peculiar nature baffled many a clergyman. No matter the situation, house rules had to be observed. Even bishops were not exempt. Much as people were free to visit him and even spend the night in his house, he expected them to abide by his routine. First, one had to arrive preferably at six and never after eight. Supper was served at seven and one was expected to be in bed at ten. The bishop did not expect to hear noise after ten o'clock. He was notorious for throwing out those who flouted these rules.

Only one man enjoyed the privilege of flouting Ndingi's rules: Archbishop John Njenga. Njenga and Ndingi had many things in common. They were both blunt, they were known for defending and helping their priests and they shared more or less the same experience with white priests. They had similar habits and thus it was only Njenga who could disrupt Ndingi's daily routine.

# CHAPTER THIRTEEN

## *Culture shock*

Like his transfer from Machakos, Ndingi's transfer from Nakuru to Nairobi came as a big disappointment to the people of Nakuru. In a terse statement signed by the Apostolic Nunciature in Nairobi on June 27, 1996, Pope John Paul II appointed Ndingi as the Coadjutor Archbishop of the Nairobi Archdiocese.

The appointment effectively gave the newly promoted Archbishop the right of succession if and when the incumbent Archbishop, then Maurice Michael Cardinal Otunga, retired. Otunga had been the Archbishop of Nairobi for twenty-five years at the time and had also occupied the lofty distinction of being the first African cardinal in Kenya. He was seventy-three at the time Ndingi was appointed and according to the Code of Canon Law 401, the retirement age for bishops is seventy-five.

Ndingi was coming to take over an archdiocese, which though, not as big in size as Nakuru was much more significant administratively and much bigger in population size. While Nakuru was regarded as the country's political hot-bed, Nairobi was the seat of political decision makers, a metropolitan See from which, it is usually widely expected, a cardinal would sprout. The Catholic Diocese of Nakuru comprising then Nakuru and Baringo districts (Kericho having been hived off and erected a diocese) had about 200,000 Catholics. It was 18,149 square kilometres in size with thirty-three parishes and ninety priests with fifty-five being diocesans and thirty-three religious. The Archdiocese of Nairobi while occupying only 3,271 square kilometres, comprised Nairobi province, Thika and Kiambu districts. It was home to an estimated Catholic population of 1.3 million. It had nearly five hundred and fifty priests, over a hundred of whom were diocesans and nearly four hundred and fifty religious. The archdiocese was founded in 1862 and boasted of over a hundred parishes.

The priests in Nakuru wanted to organise a demo against the move but the Vicar General then shot down the idea saying that that was not the way the Catholic Church handled such matters. The people were, however, not quietened. There was grumbling informed by a weird expectation that the move would be rescinded.

But as Nakuru mourned, Catholics in other parts of the country were not surprised. First Cardinal Otunga was retiring. Who would be the one to replace him? It has always been taken as a given that the archbishop of the capital city is the most visible and the seniormost of all the other bishops. In the case of Cardinal Otunga, that was, in a way, true. The expectation that whoever would be the new Archbishop of Nairobi would automatically be made cardinal or assume a higher position in the hierarchy was informed by this.

At this time, Ndingi had distinguished himself as the most vocal Catholic bishop and probably the best known. Further, it was also a time of political hiccups with agitation for constitutional review and greater democracy taking centre stage. With Ndingi, the irreverent, irascible and implacable fighter coming to Nairobi, the Catholic voice would boom and thunder

## Culture shock

with a fiercer urgency. His transfer and promotion to the capital city after twenty four years in Nakuru made headlines in all the papers. As the faithful celebrated, politicians were heard to ask, "Why Ndingi?" They knew one thing: with his coming to Nairobi the thorn that had been so troublesome could only become sharper and more poisonous.

The country then waited for the fighter of justice to assume the highest Catholic seat in the Archdiocese of Nairobi. The priests of the archdiocese knew the bishop as a moral crusader. But now that he had been promoted and brought to their diocese, they needed to know how he was as a bishop. Many made quick enquiries about the man's relationship with his priests in Nakuru, the nature of the man and his disposition as a bishop. The only consistent thing they got was, "check out his temper." Anything else was largely circumstantial. However, as some confided in these authors, they got to know a humble, understanding bishop.

After a quick "run" on his files, the priests prepared to welcome Ndingi. He was escorted all the way up to the border between Nairobi and Rift Valley province by the priests of Nakuru and it was a sad send off as they saw their hero leave for another land.

On arrival in Nairobi, Ndingi was greeted with pomp and fanfare. Many wanted to see the man who had caused such a ruckus in Nakuru in person. Some wanted to touch him. The government watched all this the way the communists watched on TV the election of Karol Wojtyla as Pope John Paul II in 1978. They knew, as the communists did, that life would not be the same again, that it would be another era of operating on a cliff-hanger. While Cardinal Otunga was a much more abstemious person and almost controversy-free, Ndingi was seen to be, quite literally, a loose cannon. He would, the political class believed, be a veritable bull in the capital's political china shop.

Questions abound: was Vatican sending a message to the regime? Was it upping the ante of what the political class believed, but the clergy denied, was a struggle between Church and State? If he could generate heat enough to make some politicians quake in their boots when he was in the country's political hotbed, how much could he do in the capital city? Who had recommended him? How had he been appointed?

There was some wishful thinking that the government should have had a say in the appointment of a new bishop for the capital city, but the Church did not operate that way, at least not in Kenya. It had its own systems of appointing bishops. In the first millennium, bishops were either elected by the people or nominated by a lay patron (emperor or King) or eventually feudal lord. Election by the people, whenever it occurred, usually led to some tumults, so election by the cathedral chapter, the clerical diocesan club, tended to replace them.[1] In the reign of the communists in Poland, the cardinals had to submit a few names to the authorities which they would approve before they went to Rome. That is how Karol Wojtyla was appointed the Archbishop of Krakow in communist Poland and went on to become Pope.

Today the second most powerful dicastery in the Vatican after the Congregation of the Doctrine of Faith, the Congregation of Bishops recommends the appointment of bishops throughout the world to the Pope. The 1917 Code of Canon Law proclaimed that while the bishops could make recommendations to the Vatican on the appointment of bishops, the Pope would always freely decide, "*eos libere nominat Pontifex Romanus* (the Pope

---

[1] Peter Hebblethewaike, *In the Vatican*, Oxford University Press

freely nominates bishops)" the code proclaimed.

The Congregation of Bishops (CoB) also deals with the division of dioceses and what is called the 'erection' of new ones. It is the body to which bishops report when they go on their quinquennial *ad limina* visits to Rome.

The process of identifying priests with qualities desired in a bishop is usually an ongoing process even if there are no vacancies. The Church is quite explicit on the qualities of a bishop. He must be a 'good pastor of souls and a teacher of faith.' The Church examines whether the candidates enjoy a good reputation, whether they are of impeccable character, irreproachable morality, endowed with the right judgement and prudence; whether they are even-tempered and of stable character, whether they firmly hold the orthodox Faith; whether they are devoted to the Apostolic See and faithful to the magisterium of the Church; whether they have a thorough knowledge of dogmatic and moral theology and Canon Law; whether they are outstanding for their piety, their spirit of sacrifice and their pastoral zeal; whether they have an aptitude for governing."

Consideration is also given to intellectual qualities, studies completed, social sense, spirit of dialogue and cooperation, openness to the signs of the times, praise-worthy impartiality, family background, health, age and inherited characteristics.

Periodically, the bishops of a province meet under the chairmanship of their archbishop to consider the names of priests who are possible candidates for the episcopacy. At the provincial meeting, a list of candidates for the episcopacy is assembled, voted on and forwarded to the apostolic nuncio. While the nuncio could nominate for bishop, someone not from this pool of candidates, and the Pope could appoint any priest he might want, most appointments generally come from these lists. When a diocese becomes vacant, the second part of the process gets underway – the search for the specific person who would fill a specific vacancy.

Local bishops also have a say in this. They are invited to put names on a list of general candidates and when a vacancy occurs, the nuncio or the apostolic delegate engages in consultations and comes up with three names: *the terna*. He writes a report extracting and synthesizing the content of the consultation and giving his own judgment. The *terna* and the report are sent to the Congregation of Bishops in Rome. No bishop sees them unless he is a member of that congregation. The report gives a description of the diocese, describes the process the nuncio went through in selecting the candidates, describes the candidates and gives the nuncio's recommendations. When the nuncio's report arrives at the Congregation of Bishops, the members discuss the appointment under the chairmanship of the prefect. The congregation then votes on the candidates and attaches its own recommendations to the report.

The final step in the appointment process takes part when the prefect of the Congregation of Bishops presents the nuncio's, the congregation's, and his own recommendations to the Pope in a private audience. The prefect summarizes the discussions of the congregation and reports any dissenting opinions. The Pope may ask for more information about the candidates, or may even ask for other candidates to be proposed. In the end however, the Pope, led by the Holy Spirit, makes the appointment.[2]

After the Pope makes his decision, the nuncio is notified, who then approaches the nominee and asks if he will accept the appointment. When the candidate accepts, Rome is notified and a date is set for the announcement. Although the process

---

[2] Fr Pat Umberger, *How a Bishop is choosen*, 2003

## Culture shock

normally takes four to eight months, it can be much shorter or much longer.

But in certain key dioceses, there have been evidence of direct papal intervention. This, as a Vatican watcher, Peter Hebblethwaite observed, is particularly true where there are 'surprises' (something that the media had not thought about). It happened in the case of Basil Hume appointed to become Archbishop of Westminster by Pope Paul VI, Josef Glemp appointed by John Paul II to succeed Cardinal Stefan Wyszynski as the primate of Poland, and Jean-Marie Lustiger promoted to become Archbishop of Paris from Orleans after serving less than a year by John Paul II in 1981.

Where then exactly was Ndingi to be placed? Like the Chancellor of England, Sir Thomas More, who looked forward to the day when, once again, bishops would be elected by the people, the government might have been wishing that that day, if ever it would come, should come faster.

In many ways, people in whom too much is invested and expected from, usually buckle under the pressure and tend to disappoint. The first few weeks of Ndingi's reign in Nairobi were somewhat tame. The much expected Shakespearean "sound and fury" was markedly different. But this was more so because he was in the shadow of his cardinal who was still the head of the archdiocese than perhaps because of possible change in his character. Still, many had immense faith in him. In Nakuru, he had given weight to the Italian saying that to be a bishop was to be the *defensor populi*, the "defender of the people" and the *defensor civitatis*, the "defender of the city" of last resort. The enactment of this role was eagerly awaited by the nation.

As happens when a new bishop is posted to another diocese, the priests compare his style of administration to that of his predecessors. In most cases, they are full of dread and unknowing and in some cases, the search for the real identity of the new bishop leads to what could be perceived as a lukewarm reception to the new bishop. Until they can understand what he likes or does not like, they can really never map him out. This was what happened to Ndingi when he came to Nairobi. The politicians were in awe, the priests yearned to understand his style of administration and the laity felt they had their man in the right place.

In Nakuru Diocese, all the clergy who had vehicles had had them registered in the name of the diocese. It was easier for the diocese to keep count of which parish had or did not have a vehicle. But when he came to Nairobi, Ndingi found that nearly all vehicles were registered in the names of their respective parishes. This presented him with his first headache. He wanted order and a clear tabulation of what the diocese owned. So he ordered the priests to surrender all the logbooks to the diocese. There was no open defiance but there was reluctance to comply with the order. The priests thought that they were up against a difficult bishop and wondered what he would do next.

"The bishop only wanted to have a better understanding of the operations of the diocese," a priest would later say, "he was neither draconian nor dictatorial."

A believer that what belonged to the Church should be in the Church's name, one of the first things he did when he came to Nairobi was to transfer the title deeds of assets to the diocese. This included some of the property that was held in the name of some of the congregation in Nairobi.

One of the things that Ndingi would not compromise on, was late night travelling among his clergy. He could not condone those who loved to drive in darkness. The priests in Nakuru

## Culture shock

understood this quite well and did all they could to ensure they never flouted the will of the bishop. When he came to Nairobi, he extended the same expectation to the priests but this was met with open reluctance. It was not possible, they argued, for them to close shop at six or seven. In Nairobi, most people worked in towns and if the priests were to minister to groups like small Christian communities they had to do this in the evenings. Driving at night was thus a part of their operations. Besides, the archdiocese was so vast that some priests had to drive for long distances through nerve-wracking traffic jams.

Ndingi did not view this as rebellion. Instead he tried to understand the priests' point of view and both priest and bishop came to an understanding. As he had written earlier on the relationship between bishops and priests, "anyone in authority should exercise it with respect, in faith, hope and above all, with love and understanding."

The priests too had to understand their bishop. Like in Nakuru, Ndingi maintained an open-door policy, dedicating one day every week to the priests. Whoever had an issue was free to go and see him. That way, a greater understanding between them was enhanced.

Gradually, they came to accept Ndingi's style. He was social and he made a point to attend their clergy meetings held every Tuesday. He extended his invitation to all and hosted them in his house where they would socialise. They could discuss matters of the diocese freely with him.

One thing they had to contend with was the bishop's temperament. Like their Nakuru counterparts, they had to learn that when the bishop was tired or unravelled he was given to spontaneous bouts of anger. One priest recalls an incident where the bishop berated him for something that a parishioner complained about. It was a busy Sunday, he recalls, and a parishioner went to receive Holy Communion. She wanted to have it served on her palm but somehow the priest did not see the outstretched palm and proceeded to place the Holy Communion on the parishioner's tongue, which she incidentally also held out.

After that, she sought out the bishop the following day and complained that the priest was rude; he had not respected her wishes on her preferred mode of receiving the Holy Communion. The Holy Communion can either be served on the palm or, more traditionally, placed on the tongue of the faithful[3]. The way the priest served it was, apparently, enough to so miff the parishioner that she had to report it to the Archbishop.

If there is one thing that Ndingi has always respected, it is the views and wishes of the faithful. So when the aggrieved parishioner tabled her complaint, Ndingi took the matter quite seriously. He called the priest and reproached him for the act.

"So serious was the bishop that I wondered if I had done something more than just unintentionally disrespect a parishioner's wishes," says the priest. After the brush, the bishop dismissed the priest from his office.

Towards lunch time the priest was surprised to see the bishop approaching him.

"Let's go for lunch, Father," he told him.

Still smarting from the tongue-lashing earlier in the day, the priest did not wish to share a table with the archbishop yet.

"No, Your Grace, just go on and have lunch, there is something that I have to finish. I will have lunch later."

The bishop looked at the priest and said, "Oh I see, go on and finish it but I'm not going for lunch without you. I will wait."

Humbled and almost embarrassed, the priest realised that

---

[3] Under reviewed Church laws, the Holy Communion can either be served on the tongue or on the palm. Previously it was served only on the tongue to a kneeling recipient.

the archbishop's anger did not run deep. Rather than have his bishop wait for him, he elected to join him for lunch immediately. At the table, only jokes and good humour prevailed.

"I came face to face with a different person," he says. "In a way, this was a challenge to me not to keep grudges."

By and by, the priests of the Nairobi Archdiocese, long used to the debonair Cardinal Otunga, started appreciating their new archbishop. They were to get pleasant surprises when Ndingi dropped at their clergy meetings and stayed with them till late. Before the year was over, he had invited them to his house for the weekly clergy meeting, respecting their wishes as to what they wanted served.

"He proved from the start that he would be a priest among priests," Fr Ndikaru says, "he was humble enough to come down to the level of the ordinary priests."

This climb down was sometimes to prove a bit too costly to his time and sometimes, his judgment. Some faithful took advantage of his accessibility to take gossip to him. Ever judicious, he sometimes would get annoyed and side with them but most of the times he mulled over the issue until he arrived at a rational decision.

The way the archbishop sometimes reacted to situations was baffling to some priests. In many cases the priests of the Nairobi Archdiocese did not know how their new shepherd would react to some situations. When they expected him to get annoyed, he never did. When they least expected him to get upset, like in the case of the priest and the parishioner, he flew off the handle.

In his early days as the Archbishop of Nairobi, he had a habit of dropping in unannounced at parishes just before the start of Mass. One Sunday, he dropped in at the St Peter Claver's Catholic Church just before the priest was about to begin Mass. When a bishop visits a parish, it is expected that he would be the one to give the homily. On this day, the priest had organised his homily and he found it difficult to cede the chance to the archbishop. The priest welcomed his bishop and humbly told him that he could only concelebrate Mass and leave the sermon to him.

"*Padre,*" responded the archbishop, "I would have loved to talk to these faithful."

"Your grace, I had already prepared the sermon, so please let me go ahead with it."

"Oh I see," he responded. The priest knew that the archbishop's request was, in fact, an order, but he did not want to consider it that way.

As they vested, the archbishop asked the priest, "*Padre*, tell me are there two bishops here?" then he smiled. The priest smiled too. The bishop concelebrated the Mass but he never gave the sermon. Afterwards, the two went and had a hearty lunch, forgetting what, if the faithful had witnessed, would have been regarded as a misunderstanding between priest and his bishop.

Nairobi for Ndingi had some surprises that he could not exactly call very pleasant. Long used to a simple life in Nakuru where he drove an old Peugeot, he found Nairobi a totally different place. A few months after he came in, a group of wealthy businessmen belonging to the archdiocese decided to welcome the archbishop in style. They were unhappy with his spartan life and so they decided to buy him a brand new vehicle. One Sunday they surprised him with their gift. It was a brand new pristine-white Mercedes Benz.

At first, the archbishop was surprised. Should he accept the gift? If not, how would he do it without annoying his benefactors? He struggled with the dilemma for some time. The media did not help matters. One columnist wrote in a daily newspaper that the Bishop was a humble servant of God and should eschew anything that would be perceived to be grandiose.

## Culture shock

He should, the columnist suggested, donate the vehicle and use the money to help the needy. There were also suggestions that the gift was meant to compromise him, given that some of the people behind it were politicians.

The archdiocese was, to be frank, in need of a vehicle. Cardinal Otunga was using an almost dilapidated Peugeot and an Audi. But some could not understand how Ndingi could be driving around in a vehicle perceived to be the grandest representative of opulence while he had always come through as a humble and simple priest.

The gift also surprised some priests who knew the archbishop as one who never attached any undue value to material property. "I was surprised to see him in a Benz," recalls Fr Kanja, "It was hard to believe he could be driven around in such a car."

Behind closed doors, Ndingi told some priests that he did not want the vehicle. But the priests and his trusted driver, Mwangi, convinced him that it would be rude to reject the gift, or to show those who had bought it for him that he did not value their benevolence. The best he could do, they advised him, was to show some gratitude.

As the debate raged on, Ndingi at first kept a studious silence. Then one day, he spoke out, explaining that the vehicle was not his personal property. It had been bought for the archdiocese of Nairobi by the friends of the archdiocese and it would be used purely for pastoral work.

That appeared to put the debate to rest. But even then, Ndingi rarely used the vehicle. He preferred the simpler Subaru which was also bought for his use by the archdiocese. He only used the Benz for long distance drives something which, according to his driver, he later came to enjoy quite immensely.

## Continuing the crusade

Because of the name he had made for himself in Nakuru, Archbishop Ndingi was a magnet for the media in Nairobi. Rarely would he celebrate Mass without a horde of press hounds waiting to record and report what he said. If they did not find anything worth reporting from the homily, they would wait for him outside the Church and throw in a question. Never one to shy from the media, he would respond to every question and it would make the evening's big story or the following morning's headlines.

The late nineties were also years of controversy. There was the clamour for the constitutional reforms and there was also the usual resistance from KANU. The civil society, Law Society of Kenya, some opposition politicians and the Church took the cue and started championing the cause for constitutional reforms. This was shortly after the 1997 General Election in which President Moi was elected for his final term. The push for constitutional reforms appeared to have died out shortly after the election and the country was settling down under a new political dispensation in which Moi would do his last term as head of state.

Just before the election there were efforts to push for a national convention to review the constitution. It was fronted by opposition politicians, key among them, Mr Kenneth Matiba and a group of civic organisations under the banner of the National Convention Executive Committee (NCEC). Matiba opted out of the election and began fronting the idea of Mass action and civil disobedience to force the government into accepting a constitutional conference. Matiba was borrowing an idea from the Philippines, where popular uprising fronted by Catholic Cardinal Jaime Sin, forced Ferdinand Marcos out of power.

Sensing pressure, the government adopted a few measures to lance the bubble of what it saw as a serious source of political discontent. First the Members of Parliament from across the entire political spectrum came together under the auspices of the Interparty Parliamentary Group (IPPG) and agreed on a programme to approach constitutional reforms. A number of reforms were actually implemented before the general election. The IPPG accord also led to the passing of an act of parliament that not only obliged the government to institute constitutional reforms but also spelt out the methods of choosing the membership of an all-inclusive constitutional review commission. This appeared to have taken the wind out of the sails of the proponents of a constitutional conference and indeed, the clergy appeared to have backed off from its crusade.

Then, out of the blues, the clergy struck back. Teaming up with other bishops, Ndingi found himself at the centre of those calling for a constitutional conference. In a tough statement to the government in February 1998, the clergymen proposed a Church-led constitutional conference which, according to their proposal would turn into a people's assembly translating into a popular, new political dispensation. The statement talked about "the reconstitution of the Kenyan State" in which the ordinary person would have a major say as to what kind of constitution they wanted.

The statement drew a vociferous round of condemnation from politicians of all shades and persuasion. *The Weekly Review* in its cover of February 27 1998, called it "Church Revolt: the clergy in new offensive against the government." President Moi described the clergymen as "revolution-minded" and strongly criticised them for what he called "waging a smear campaign against the government." Kalonzo Musyoka, then Minister for Education and Manpower Development, termed the bishop's call for external intervention an insult to the country's sovereignty. The Attorney General, Amos Wako, issued a swift rejoinder rubbishing the bishops' statement and adding that "the constitutional review exercise must be approached in a cool manner, with sobriety of mind and a clear vision for the future of this country and all its inhabitants."

The bishops achieved one thing: they managed to bring the review agenda back on chart but they lacked the push that was required to elevate it onto a platform where the government could take action.

# CHAPTER FOURTEEN

## *Reconstructing the African face of Christ*

The fire that was burning in Ndingi's belly while he was in Nakuru was not very much in evidence in Nairobi. Had this leopard changed his spots? The one thing about Ndingi is that he is so honest about his feelings that he sometimes does not take into consideration how others take his sentiments. Even in the episcopate, he was known to shoot from the hip, speak his mind and air opinions that sometimes went against the grain of those who were present. When he believed in something, no one could distract him.

One of the things that Ndingi believed in was a recognition of the African marriage customs and its acceptance by the Church. He believed that the Church should take cognisance of the diversity of the cultures of its faithful while also preserving its teachings and try and incorporate some of them into the liturgy.

These views were laid bare in 1994 during the African Synod in the Vatican. The assembly held between April and May gathered African bishops to advise on the agenda of the Catholic Church's evangelising mission in Africa in the next millennium. The synod awareness was part of a series of synods held in the same period across the world. Europe was scheduled to hold its synod the October of that year.

Even before the synod began, a lot of views were being exchanged in the media. It was the first gathering of African bishop-delegates in modern history. While it was generally agreed that the synod could hardly be seen as "any loosening of the apron strings of Rome", as the *Daily Nation* put it, it gave Africa a unique opportunity to make its voice heard.

The synod came at a time when African bishops felt that since the Catholic Church in Africa had grown exponentially, it also had the ability to be responsible for itself. There were calls for an African council which would do for Africa what the second Vatican council did for the whole Catholic Church. These calls had started since the mid 1970s. The council, it was proposed, would be established on African soil to deliberate on, make decisions for and legislate for the African Church[1]. In his visits to Africa, Pope John Paul II had hinted that such a council was possible. There was then wide expectations that the Vatican might just establish the council during the reign of John Paul.

But instead of the council, the Pope announced in 1989 that there would be a special assembly of the Synod of Bishops. This is primarily a consultative body called by the Pope to assist and advise him. The function of the synod of bishops according to Canon 343 is to discuss the matters proposed to it and set forth recommendations. The Canon Law makes it clear that the synod's function is not to settle matters or draw up decrees "unless the Roman Pontiff has given it deliberative power in certain cases" in which case the power to ratify the decisions of the synod lie with the Pope.

---

[1] Knight Phillips: The African Synod in Rome, 1994 Consequences for Catholicism

## The African Synod

The African Synod was then being asked to discuss the theme of evangelisation in the African context. According to the outline document of the synod known as the *Lineamenta* there were going to be five chapters on the tasks of evangelisation:

- proclamation of the Good News
- inculturation
- dialogue
- justice and peace
- the means of social communication

These themes formed the framework for all the subsequent preparations for the synod, the synod itself and for the post-synodal documents.

In the *Lineamenta* were eighty-one questions such as: do you consider inculturation as urgent and necessary for the Church in Africa, or to what extent have the modern means of transport and social communication affected closer interactions between adherents of different religions in your area? How has this affected the Church's mission of evangelisation?

These questions were sent out to the Episcopal Conferences of Africa and some dioceses discussed them at the parish level with their faithful. There was a response of over ninety per cent to the *Lineamenta*. It is these responses that shaped the *Instrumentum Laboris* – the working document of the synod.

The synod would start on April 10 to May 8, 1994. There was some disappointment that it had not been held in Africa but it was said then that Rome had been the preferred venue by the majority of the African bishops.

The immediate fruit of the nearly month-long synod was two-fold: one was a series of proposals to the Pope, the other was a public statement, "the message of the synod," addressed to the Church in Africa but mainly a public document to be accessed by whomever was interested.

One issue that took centre stage was inculturation. There was a prevailing feeling that the liturgy was not close enough to the people and was, perhaps, foreign to them. In order to bring it closer, the Catholic Church in Africa had to speak and act in a way that would resonate with its followers.

The aim of inculturation was to ensure authenticity and depth of faith in the African Christian, "to heal cultural alienation, to bridge the gap between faith and life and thus resolve the many instances of 'spiritual schizophrenia and double life affecting many of the peoples of Africa," as the *Lineamenta* put it.

This is where Bishop Ndingi's paper, which some termed candid and a bit controversial, was presented. Above all, the bishop came through both in the synod and after as a fierce defender of African values and African way of life in a way few people knew him.

A call for inculturation of the elements that informed the African way of life while not going beyond the ambit of the Church's teaching, created quite a stir and some controversy at the synod more than the other four listed themes. It was felt that authentic inculturation could not ignore the political, economic and social contexts in which the Church in Africa operated. Cultures were constantly transforming and much of the engine of transformation came from the political, economic and social forces which affect the people in one way or the other. The results which would develop from the synod both in terms of the relationship between the Roman centre of the Church and the African local churches would be deemed as an inculturated ecclesiology.

There was a feeling among the bishops and the African people that the dynamism of their culture was not taken into account in the operations of the Church. The family, for instance rose as a key issue. While the African family was applauded, fears about its future were also expressed. While Christian marriage was affirmed, there was intense debate about the status of customary marriages in Africa.

There was a caucus of bishops who rose up in fierce defense of the African traditional families. The Archbishop of Dakar Senegal, Hyacinthe Cardinal Thiandoum (now deceased) raised the issue thus:

> Marriage and family need to be looked at more closely, in order to recover and promote the precious values of the traditional African family. This could be a great contribution to finding an effective response to the crisis of the family in many modern societies. We need greater appreciation for our various customary laws of marriage and serious effort to harmonise them with church laws on marriage.

Cardinal Thiandoum found an indefatigable ally in Bishop Ndingi but while Thiandoum was more diplomatic and subtle in his presentation, Ndingi was more pointed and forceful positing that there was an "Eucharistic famine" in Africa because of the Church's refusal to give African customary marriages canonical value:

> Many of our Christian faithful have finalised their marriage according to the African customs of their own tribe but for different reason they have not yet come to the Church for sacramental marriage...In the meantime they are considered by the Church to be living in concubinage because their traditional marriage has no canonical value. The consequence is that they are deprived of the reception of the sacraments, which, in the expression of some of our priests, leads to a "Eucharistic famine" of many Catholics in our parishes.

Ndingi suggested that the Church should adapt Canon Law to African culture. This flew in the face of the expectations of the Congregation for Divine Worship and the sacraments which had issued a preemptive document stating that the topic of inculturation could only be considered within the control of the Church.

But Ndingi argued that, to combat the "Eucharistic famine" the Church had the right to make changes in the form of the sacraments *salva illorum substantia* (providing the substance is kept) as the Council of Trent put it. Ndingi argued that no precise form of Christian marriage emerges from the New Testament. The Canonical form of Catholic marriage has its origins in Roman civil law. Its main components are the exchange of vows and the moment of consent from both parties. But there is an argument that consent can be expressed in other ways, through a process rather than at a precise point in time. Ndingi explained:

> Traditional marriage has a civil and social value in our African societies. Those who perform it enjoy all the rights and obligations of real spouses in the eyes of the state. Even in the eyes of the Church, the customary marriage of a non-Christian couple who want to be baptised is recognised as a valid marriage and no further marriage is required after their baptism.

He argued that family pressures prevent Catholics from going through the Christian marriage ceremony, though they may want it. "It ought not to be beyond the wit of theologians to discover a pastoral solution that would harmonize Christian and customary marriage," argued Ndingi.

While acknowledging that Christianity was independent of all cultures, Ndingi argued that it must, nevertheless, insert itself into all cultures in order to purify and sanctify them.

There was widespread recognition that the best-organised bishops at the synod were from Kenya. Writing in the *National Catholic Reporter*, Peter Hebblethwaite acknowledged that the Kenyan bishops shared out the topics in advance, made good use of the theologians of the Catholic University of Eastern Africa and provided a sketch for what could be the final propositions. Hebblethwaite observed that Ndingi, for instance tackled competently the most fundamental problem at the synod, "marriage" and dared suggest that a post-synodal commission be constituted on the topic since he did not think that the synod could exhaustively deal with the question.

After the synod, Ndingi wrote a paper outlining what was deliberated on, making a lucid elaboration of the rationale behind the synod and pushing his argument further that the Catholic Church in Africa had to take in some components of the African traditions.

"How is it ," he asked, "that after more than a hundred years of Christianity, there are still many traditional values that are obviously and intrinsically opposed to Christian gospel values, and that the former outweigh the latter in day to day life?"

His contention was that since the missionaries had brought the gospel to Africa, it would be unrealistic of the Africans to expect them to play a key role in inculturation. Missionaries, he posited, come and go and can only preach the Gospel as they know it and live it and cannot be expected to carry out the process of inculturation for the Africans. "It is our challenge and our privilege to present the African face of Christ," he argued.

To him the fight to have the Church present "the African face of Christ" was much more than the introduction of mere traditional components. He saw inculturation as the incarnation of Christ within a culture. "Christ," he said, "makes his home in the culture, and the culture finds a house in Christ. The culture is a house in Christianity."

Ndingi described inculturation a"bringing sanity to Christianity", to recognise that our culture was open to accept and absorb Christianity and also that the Africans found their belief in the presence of their ancestors in a situation akin to the doctrine of the communion of saints.

The idea of one faith brought to the peoples of Africa from lands far and diverse was upheld in Africa, he argued. But Africans were very slow to encourage any sort of native art in their liturgy and in many instances were even fearful to celebrate their worship with African dance and rhythm:

> The approved musical instrument for worship was the organ. This was second nature, say in Germany where there was a centuries' old tradition, from Bach and Standel, in organ recital; and also the magnificent cathedrals and churches vying with each other in acoustic excellence. There was transcendence and sacred hypnotism in this. Our transcendence and sacred hypnotism is in the rhythmic pulse of African life. We have our whispering drums, talking drums, singing drums, capable of evoking every human sentiment from awe to exhilaration...we also have our stringed instruments like the nyatiti, the litungu and the obakano..."[2]

Was the bishop being an implacable Africanist or where was he drawing his passion from? In many ways, the African synod was one of the biggest milestones, according to Ndingi, in the Catholic Church in Africa. So forceful was he in its defense that when a missionary priest, Fr Brian Hearne, wrote a critical piece in the newspapers about the synod, Ndingi's hackles were immediately raised.

---

[2] Bishop Ndingi: Synod of Bishops, Special Assembly for Africa, September 1994.

Fr Hearne had criticised the synod by asserting that the synod achieved nothing and that the African bishops were silenced during the synod. He further alleged that most topics like celibacy, the code of Canon Law about marriage, the liturgical rules of the Roman rite, political involvement of priests and sisters and the population explosion were not discussed openly.[3]

Ndingi wrote a strongly worded rejoinder published in the same paper's edition of June 19, 1994. In it, he accused Fr Hearne of styling himself up as the African bishops' spokesman and spreading falsehoods about the synod. "Why does he set himself up as a spokesman for Africans in a way which is so insulting to them?" he asked, "His letter shows as little respect for us Africans as for the truth."

Ndingi appeared stung by Fr Hearne's allegation that the African bishops had been gagged at the synod. To this, Ndingi replied that the bishops spoke clearly for themselves and their people and that they did not need Fr Hearne, who was not present at the Synod, to speak for them.

"If disrespect has been shown to the Church in Africa as he contends, it is certainly not by anything that happened at the synod in Rome. It is rather by false accounts of what is supposed to have happened like that by Fr Hearne."

A number of people wrote in the following days to castigate Fr Hearne and support Ndingi. Apparently the African synod had a lot of supporters and most shared Ndingi's views on inculturation.

Still, questions were being asked. Why, one would ask, was Ndingi so enamoured with the topic of church and African customary marriage? To begin with, Ndingi's parents were not

---

[3] *Sunday Nation*, May 21st 1994

initially Christians. Ndingi was the first Christian in his family. But even as he grew up he saw and respected the cultures of his people.

"Everyone has something to offer. Every culture is valuable," he says. He therefore believed that one can practice traditional rites and still not be far from God. Thus, he deeply felt that the "problem of harmonising traditional marriage with the sacrament must not be put in second place."

In some ways, the bishop felt responsible for the many souls who yearned to be in communion with the Church but who, because of their way of life could not be admitted into such communion. "As a Eucharistic people" he told a congregation of delegates to the African synod at the Holy Family Basilica on April 4, 1994, just before the synod began, "we cannot let our conscience rest whilst so many of our brothers and sisters who are deeply committed to the Church, are denied access to the Eucharistic table of the Lord because of their marital status. What can we African church leaders do to help our people here?"

His contention was that the African who becomes a Christian does not necessarily have to negate himself but drags along the age-old values with him. Quoting Pope Paul VI, Ndingi averred that "The teaching of Jesus Christ and his redemption are, in fact the complement, the renewal, and the bringing to perfection, of all that is good in human tradition. And that is why the African who becomes a Christian does not disown himself, but takes up the age-old values of tradition "in spirit and in truth."

# CHAPTER FIFTEEN

## *The thorny issue of celibacy*

Up to this day, there is nothing that pains Ndingi more than the willful violation of priestly vows and the failure or refusal of those who cannot keep on with the priestly vow of celibacy to seek dispensation in the normal, accepted ways.

On many occasions, Ndingi spoke about this issue at length. At every priestly ordination, he exhorted the priests to uphold the vow of celibacy and live up to their calling as the Lord's servants. No matter what the culture, celibacy, Ndingi emphasised was an individual personal gift and calling. "It is a personal burden that is light, if we take the adequate means to protect it," he told a congregation at a priestly ordination at Tangaza College on November 28, 1992, "we see its beauty in prayer. It is the pearl of great price that we have found."

In spite of the instances when the vow of celibacy has been wantonly broken by some clergy, Ndingi believed and still does, that celibacy was possible even in the most outrageously difficult circumstances. But he also acknowledged that celibate life is for the few, the brave few, "for those who can accept, for those who can lead a disciplined life."

A key component to leading a fullsome celibate life was prayer. This is something he affirmed repeatedly when he met priests or delivered homilies at their ordination. Priestly celibacy was for those who watched and prayed and those who oblated themselves fully to a life of service of God. "We cannot serve God and the world," he told priests at the Hekima Jesuit School of Theology on February 17$^{th}$, 1993, "if we look back once our hands are on the plough we are not fit for the Kingdom, for the mission entrusted to us, for the call we have answered."

Yet, the Archbishop believed that even those priests who were not able to keep up with their priestly vows were more in need of help than condemnation. But before the help was offered, he demanded honesty and forthrightness among those who genuinely sought it.

"A priest," Ndingi once told an audience of rectors, "remains human and is beset by temptations like any other Christian." "A priest," he told them, "is liable to fail and to fail badly." But this does not mean that he does not have a vocation. "St Peter," he stressed, "was not removed from among the twelve after he denied Christ. One who is obviously trying to respond to God's love is to be encouraged."

Many priests are forever appreciative of the help they got from Ndingi whenever their vocations were threatened. Fr Kanja says, "Ndingi was especially helpful to those priests whose vocations were threatened and who sought help from him. He never condemned. He tried to help."

But what he could not countenance were priests who refused to acknowledge that they had a problem or did not attempt to seek help for it. Much as he believed that a life of prayer would help the priests stick to the straight and the narrow, he also believed that those who genuinely recognised they had a problem and desired to be helped, either through counselling or prayer, should be accorded that help:

## The thorny issue of celibacy

> A great indication of a person's sincerity is to enquire whether he is open in his dealings with his bishop and seminary staff. Is he being true to himself? Or is he secretive and hidden? If the latter stands, then he must be helped to change and be shown that all need guidance and direction which are possible only if he takes the risk to share.[1]

He stressed continually the need for church leaders to listen to those in need of guidance. They should be treated with kindness and their leaders should be always available to see them and listen to them. "Make your home available to them if and when they need to be there," he once told fellow bishops and religious superiors. "Often-times when priests and or religious persons come to us, all they want is to be listened to with an open mind and a sincere heart." However, he always encouraged those who felt that they could not cope, to seek dispensation, to go about things the correct way.

Before priests can get to be ordained, proper choices must be made, vocations must be nurtured in the correct way and the major seminaries must inculcate values in the seminarians which would enable them lead celibate lives as per the requirements of the Church. At the seminary stage, careful discernment is critical. Only candidates found fit and capable of developing in the vocation should be recruited and assisted to develop further.

"When there is doubt about a candidate's suitability, he should be advised and helped to find his vocation in the world," he told a meeting of vocation promoters in Nairobi on October 24, 1993.

But a candidate thus advised should never be made to feel rejected or useless. Every assistance, he urged, should be given to

---

[1] *The Idea of Vocation: The problem of selection and discernment in the context of E. Africa*, by Bishop Ndingi, 1989.

make them adapt to their new environment. Physical deformity, he stressed should not, as a rule, be reason for rejecting a candidate. Similarly, those electing a life of celibacy should never consider celibacy as a negative denial of marriage but rather "total acceptance of Christ, readiness to live and serve others."

The promotion of vocations, he believed, should be undertaken with all the seriousness necessary. Only the best and mature priests in the diocese should be entrusted with the promotion of vocations, those whose lives mirrored the life of Christ.

"What techniques did Christ adapt in his mission?" he asked vocation promoters, "The first technique which shouts from every page of the Gospel is not so much what Christ did but what He was, not so much in his apostolic activity but his apostolic way of life—his humility, his poverty and his readiness to do his Father's will."

He thus expected his priests to set a good example to those they led. Though he never voiced it publicly he expected priests in the Nairobi Archdiocese to always wear their clerical collar as was the custom in Nakuru. Though it was not a hard and fast rule, the donning of the collar was, to him a testimony to one's pride as a servant of the Lord, an example of distinction between those who lead and the flock they lead. In his first days as Archbishop of Nairobi, many priests admit to thinking that they were offending to the archbishop if they appeared before him without the clerical collar. Much later they got used to the idea that their bishop was more concerned about how they lived their priestly life and carried out their pastoral duties than what they wore.

In fact, while addressing a seminar for rectors and spiritual directors of Eastern and Southern Africa at St Thomas Senior

Seminary, in Langata, on 28th July 1989, Ndingi stressed the need for priests not to set themselves apart from the communities they serve by way of dress, titles or living facilities.

"Sometimes the way of dress, titles, separate living facilities which are generally a part of a priest's lifestyle, while often helpful, need not be necessary to the priest's role in the community and sometimes may be a hindrance in his work," he said.

But he also acknowledged that there is a subtly calculated, maybe diabolical, tendency to secularise the priest. Too often, too many priests have succumbed to the trend; have become 'one of the lads' in dress and recreation and overall behaviour. Thus, his belief has been that the priest's attire must befit their priestly office and purpose, even on their off-days:

> The priest by tradition is a 'signum elevatum' (an elevated sign.) He is a beacon to beckon others to follow safely on. If the sign that should stand out is lowered and no longer seen, then it has failed in its purpose. That is what has happened too often of late. The young Church in Africa needs priests, an authentic few committed to Christ and his values, rather than a shiftless many who bend to every permissive breeze and are grateful to be 'with it.[2]

Priests, he insisted must remain priests all the way. But what, even as he entered the last decade of his episcopate, saddened him was that some priests did not want to be priests in that sense of totality. "Some have already succumbed to a level of compromise between sacred pledge and sad performance," he says, "they want to be priestly, not *sana* (very much) but *kidogo tu* (just a little) as if there ever was a 'no-man's land' between the commitment Christ demands and the compromise man commends."

---

[2] "Why be a priest?" A sermon by Ndingi Mwana a' Nzeki

Yet, he was always appreciative of the fact that priests also led a difficult life in their efforts to uphold their vows. He was especially sensitive to anything that threatened priestly celibacy but those who ever had an opportunity to lay bare their lives to their bishop recall that Ndingi was always supportive. He tried to help them in the best way he could, sometimes even transferring them to far away places just to separate them from the women threatening their priestly life.

In the early 1990s, Father Peter Mbuchi, an upcoming, young intelligent priest, was stationed in Nakuru Diocese. Mbuchi had had his measure of problems since his seminary days. He was a seminarian in Nyeri when he was accused of leading a strike in the seminary and he was expelled. But some of the priests there had faith in him and still believed he would make a good priest. His spiritual adviser, Fr Remigio Dalsanto for one believed that a young man, endowed with exemplary talents should not be let go off the seminary because of an infraction he probably had never intended. There was only one bishop he knew who could be willing to listen to the young man and even offer him a chance. He called up Ndingi in Nakuru and explained the situation.

"Let me see the young man," he told Fr Dalsanto, even though a letter sent by the rector had already damned Mbuchi to almost irredeemable levels.

Arriving in Nakuru one morning, Mbuchi met the bishop. He was jovial and at the same time had a strict countenance, Mbuchi recalls.

"He had this way of making you feel at ease," he recalls, "I felt I could open up to him."

For close to an hour, Ndingi listened to Mbuchi. Somehow he was struck by the young man's sincerity and determination to become a priest.

## The thorny issue of celibacy

"This is my candidate," he heard him say.

From then onwards, Mbuchi became a seminarian in the Catholic Diocese of Nakuru. After being accepted back, Mbuchi wrote Ndingi a letter expressing his gratitude "Sooner or later," he wrote, "you will realise that I am not the kind of person you have been told I am."

From then onwards, Ndingi and Mbuchi were one. "I believed my personality and his danced to each other," Mbuchi was later to say.

When Mbuchi became a priest, the chemistry between him and Ndingi continued to flourish. Mbuchi found himself undertaking tasks that required full trust of the bishop. When Ndingi wanted something done, he sent for Mbuchi. When he wanted to replace white missionaries with Africans, he always sent Mbuchi to take over. In many ways, Mbuchi was able to execute Ndingi's will and plans almost faultlessly. In cases where he was supposed to take over from other missionaries, he was able to make the transition and at the same time launch the Church at a higher level.

Ndingi thought he had found his man in Mbuchi. He trusted him fully and saw him as his son to the extent that the other priests thought that Ndingi favoured him. So much did Ndingi trust Mbuchi that in 1986 he made him a representative of all the diocese priests in Moshi at the General Assembly and twenty-five years anniversary of AMECEA. In Mbuchi's own words, "the bishop had fantasies about what I would become. He saw me as his spiritual son, as someone to whom he would pass the mantle."

Yet, much as he trusted the priest, Ndingi was afraid to let Mbuchi know how he felt about him even as he told everyone else what a wonderful priest Mbuchi was.

At one point, he wanted Mbuchi to go to America to study sociology. But Mbuchi was too much in love with his work and was not ready to go. Instead, the bishop sent Fr Patrick Kanja.

Fr Mbuchi was, however, to find himself in some inauspicious circumstances. In the course of his work, he met a nun with whom some intimacy developed. The nun was in charge of schools in the area that Mbuchi was administering. The relationship blossomed and in 1990, the nun got pregnant with Mbuchi's child.

When Ndingi came to know of it, he sent for the priest and they discussed the matter openly. Mbuchi told the bishop that he wanted to quit priesthood on account of what had happened.

"Why?" the bishop asked in consternation, "because of the relationship?"

Clearly, Ndingi did not know the whole truth. Then Mbuchi dropped what he thought was a bombshell,

"You see," he told him, "the lady is heavy with my child."

Ndingi looked up as he is wont to when in deep thought. He looked at the priest and said. "Yes, you have done wrong. But you are not the first one to fall into that kind of problem. You are still a priest."

The two continued debating the issue. According to Mbuchi, Ndingi talked to him as only a father would. In many ways, he believed that the Church should not be denied the services of such a priest because of the sin of the flesh.

Soon after, Mbuchi took some time off to spend thirty days interrogating his soul in an exercise called Ignitian Exercises (so named after St Ignatius). The exercises were conducted under Fr Cecily McGarry SJ who was Mbuchi's spiritual advisor. He spent the days reading the book of Job. Peharps equating his tribulations with those of Job.

## The thorny issue of celibacy

Afterwards, Ndingi, determined to save Mbuchi's priesthood sent him to a remote parish in Mombasa where he had to work with very difficult missionary priests. But despite these efforts the relationship between Fr Mbuchi and the nun continued. Ndingi, who had thought that Mbuchi would, at least, forget her got to know that the relationship was continuing. He had a perfect intelligence network. All his life, Ndingi had maintained a close relationship with the Masses and with his priests. He would drop by a convent here and a parish there. That is how he got to know that Fr Mbuchi had not broken off the relationship. He called him for a chat and Ndingi encouraged him to leave the woman and continue with his vocation. He could see the will in the priest yet there was a weakness that prevented him from acting. Ndingi hoped to act on that weakness and eventually prevail over the priest. Later Mbuchi went to America to create distance between himself and the nun and at the same time lend her support.

But none of that was working. Defeated, Mbuchi felt he had to quit. "There was no way I was going to abandon that lady," he says, "I felt the Church expected me to reject her and the child. Something, I could not do."

Ndingi still believed that Mbuchi should not quit. Even after Mbuchi wrote to the Vatican explaining his circumstances, the bishop advised him not to send the letter. When Mbuchi finally wrote to the Vatican asking to be laicized, Ndingi felt betrayed.

Ndingi's position on the celibacy was quite strong. While he would encourage priests to rise above temptations, there were some things he was unequivocal on: "Priests who have fathered children should never be allowed to live a double life. It is either celibacy (service to Church) or family but not both," he maintained. His insistence that Mbuchi go on with his ministry was therefore a contradiction in terms. But it showed how much he believed in Mbuchi, his transgressions against his vows notwithstanding.

Upon Mbuchi's decision to leave the ministry, Ndingi underwent a period of turmoil, those who worked with him say, "It was as though something died in him," recalls Fr Mirango, "it was as though he had lost a son."

On February 19, 1994 Ndingi wrote a heart-rending letter to Mbuchi expressing his regret at his decision to leave the priesthood.

> Dear Peter,
>
> It is with deep regret and sadness that I write to acknowledge receipt of your letter dated 8th February, 1994. I have read your letter and I see the unfortunate decision you have reached to leave priesthood. With effect from the moment you receive this letter, you cease to practise your priesthood except as stated in Can.976. The obligation for celibacy remains until such time as laicization is requested and dispensation granted. I take this opportunity to assure you of my continued prayers and I will always be available to assist you in any way I can...

On February 23, 1994, Ndingi wrote to all the parishes of the Catholic Diocese of Nakuru, all Kenya Catholic bishops and the Apostolic pro-Nuncio informing them that Fr. Mbuchi "had decided to resign from the priestly ministry (a decision he had taken) after much prayer and reflection."

Ndingi further wrote to Mbuchi in July, 1994 asking him to write a much fuller statement in which he would give an account of his life and also his inner journey which had led him to where he was:

> The reasons for which you are asking to leave the priesthood and be dispensed from celibacy, which you have summarised in your letter to the Holy Father, should be elaborated and clearly explained in this statement. Be very honest in this account and

do not be too brief in describing your inner journey especially, so that those who have to judge your request in Rome may have sufficient grounds to make a sound judgment and hopefully recommend a dispensation. At the same time you should state only what is true without any exaggeration..[3]

At the time Ndingi was writing this letter, he had seemingly given up on saving Mbuchi's priesthood. A number of letters had been exchanged between the priest and his Ordinary and despite Ndingi's best efforts, Mbuchi had decided to leave. In his letter to Rome asking for laicization, Mbuchi stated that "for over six years I have been tormented by the conflict between the official teaching of the Catholic Church on the priesthood and my own experience as a sexually active person."

He further went on to say that after parenting two children and having always preached responsible parenthood and against discrimination and suffering of children and single mothers, "I feel it a requirement of honesty that I should not preach water and drink wine. I have therefore publicly accepted my parenthood and wish to identify myself with these children and their mother, Mary Gertrude Kasiva, without remorse, guilt, shame or fear."

Even as he left the priesthood, Mbuchi wrote one last letter to Ndingi, lamenting a few incidents when he felt let down by the Ordinary but acknowledging that the bishop was 'an honest man who would never intentionally say or do anything to hurt another person.' In the letter, Mbuchi's bitterness came to the fore and he sought to lay down a few incidences that were both accusatory and condemnatory of the bishop, "yet my honour and respect for you will always endure." The letter was personal in nature but it also underscored the kind of relationship that Ndingi had with his priests, even those with whom they differed

---

[3] Letter to Mbuchi, 21st July 1994

fundamentally. Like Mbuchi they were forced to acknowledge the "atmosphere of openness" in which the bishop sought to ferret out matters.

Mbuchi was eventually granted laicization after thirteen years of priesthood and left the Church in 1994. He married Mary Gertrude Kasiva at Mwangaza Spiritual Jesuit House on December 31, 1999 at a low key ceremony presided over by his spiritual advisor, Fr McGarry.

Ndingi was evidently in agony after this. Had he invested too much in Mbuchi? Couldn't his ministry have been saved? Ndingi believed that celibacy should not be used to deny the Church the services of such priests. He agonised for days about Mbuchi. Ndingi still believes in his heart of hearts that Mbuchi is still a priest even though he left the Church.

The case of Mbuchi revealed a man who was fiercely loyal to the Church but who, at the same time, was still rooted to his African roots. Ndingi's initial refusal to let Mbuchi go, his frantic efforts to save his priesthood and his perorations about the need to uphold celibacy and the importance of waking up and walking when one stumbled upon the hurdles of one's vocation, reveals a man who not only deeply cared about his priests but who also felt that African priests were operating in peculiar circumstances. He believed in the abrogation of celibacy, but also accepted the Church's position on it.

Yet he also believed that it was the local Ordinary's duty to cultivate a good relationship with a priest. "If there is no misunderstanding between the bishop and priest," he often said, "then even when some priests went away, they would still come back." In his reign in Nairobi, he accepted back a priest who went to the USA to study but failed to return after his studies. One day Ndingi was shocked to receive a call from the priest.

"If I came back, would you agree to see me?" the priest asked.

"Come back and see me," he told him.

"Will you accept me back?" he sought assurance.

"Just come and see me. I'm your bishop and father."

The priest came back and after he listened to him, Ndingi accepted him into the archdiocese and posted him to a parish in the eastern deanary. As this book was being written, the priest was happily carrying out his pastoral duties at a parish in the Nairobi Archdiocese.

Ndingi was a firm believer, as the Mbuchi case amply demonstrates, that the Church must harness priests. In fact, he wrote a letter to the nuncio on November 28, 1983 outlining the possible causes why diocesan priests were leaving the ministry and offering suggestions to help the Church ring-fence them. Other than lack of vocation, he enumerated some of the possible reasons as being lack of understanding between the priest and the Ordinary, lack of fatherly spirit on the part of the Ordinary, disagreement between the two and the Ordinary appointing a priest alone and away from colleagues hence paving the way for the priest to fall into the wrong company.

"It is so hurting to see a good priest and who is sincerely seeking help from those who should give, getting turned down. Is it better to keep a priest who is not happy in his own diocese and eventually see him leave the ministry or is it better to let him transfer and keep happy and in the ministry. If this option was or is given there are some priests who would have remained in their ministry."[4]

---

[4] Private letter to Nuncio, 28th November 1983.

# CHAPTER SIXTEEN

## *Fighting the culture of death*

In his years in Nakuru, Ndingi spent virtually all his time fighting for social justice and human rights. In his early years in Nairobi he plunged headlong into a new fight: that of the use of the condom and the unnatural methods of family planning.

He railed against what Pope John Paul II called the culture of death and almost elevated what was initially a low key fight for the Church's dogma to a new level of what was to be seen as religious activism. He took on the government on this matter and ensured that he never wasted an opportunity to talk about contraception and the Church's stand on it.

Quoting liberally from Pope Paul VI's *Humanae Vitae*, Ndingi made it clear that just as he had fought social injustice in the Rift Valley, he would take no prisoners where the issue of contraception was concerned.

He believed that he was fighting against moral erosion and a society which had accepted moral relativism in place of the Church's teachings and which was in urgent need of salvation. Our age, he never tired of reminding those who cared to listen, had undergone profound sexual revolution, a widespread destruction of the basic values inherent in human life.

While acknowledging the genuine desire of the government to control population growth in order to engender development, he believed that attempts to introduce contraceptives, even to the youth and the unmarried was a move orchestrated by outsiders hell-bent on destroying the moral fabric of the Kenyan society. These agencies were waving the banner of Kenya's soaring birthrate to create a market for their products.

He believed that the country was being used as a dumping ground for dangerous medication which had been considered unsuitable in the developed world.

Some saw Ndingi as a man too steeped in dogma to clearly see the challenges the country was facing in terms of uncontrolled population growth. But those behind his crusade within the Catholic Church saw a man unrelenting in his cause and a gallant defender of the Church's teachings.

But Ndingi pushed his crusade to polemical levels arguing not just against unnatural methods of family planning but the very concept of family planning as a means to control population and spur growth. Quoting philosophers and theologians, Ndingi argued that population growth was never known to be the cause of famines. "We are told that a rising population outstrips the means available," he told a congregation at Asumbi Teachers' College on March 26, 1988, "but is it not also true that the few accumulate more and more at the expense of the poor?"

To argue that leaner populations allowed societies to escape the perils of nature, he said, was fallacious. Quoting a population expert, Dr E.F Schumacher, Ndingi posed: "Famine has often killed people off, of course; the more people there are, the more it can kill. But this number has seldom or never been the cause of the famine."

While acknowledging that the population problem was a

real one, he argued that it was wrong for societies to associate it with the general desire to have sexual fun while avoiding the consequences. "Sexual permissiveness means that contraceptives are an incitement to pursue sex as an end in itself," he said.

Fashioning out his crusade as a war between the developed and the less developed worlds, Ndingi believed that many drug companies conveniently omitted to tell the doctors about the drug dangers and others sold banned drugs under different names. He argued that in the US the number of lawsuits brought against some of the drug companies had made them, in some cases, to withdraw some products from the market. But these products still continued to be sold in the less developed countries.

Furthermore, some of the products, notably the Intra-uterine Device (IUD) was designed not to prevent contraception but to destroy already formed human life and could only then be an abortifacient.

Ndingi preached against female sterilization, vasectomy and the use of the condom as being anti-nature and unchristian and advocated for the use of natural family planning method. Many a time, the media made fun of him because of the way he pronounced the word condom – '*koondom*'. So disgusted was he with the condom, they said, that he did not even know how to pronounce its name correctly.

Ndingi's opposition to unnatural methods of family planning was in concert with the stand of the KEC of which Ndingi was chairman, which, in 1985 issued a strongly worded statement against the liberal use of contraceptives and condoms calling it an "affront to the dignity of our youth and to the respect that is due to them."

Yet, these were tenebrous times as far as the issue of family planning went, not just for the Church in Kenya but the entire Catholic Church globally. About the same time the debate was taking shape in Kenya a world population conference in Mexico in 1984 had debated the matter at length and stated flatly that abortion was not a legitimate means of family planning though it fell short of condemning family planning entirely. This debate was to go on culminating in the 1994 World Conference on Population and Development in Cairo.

As in Cairo and Mexico, the Church in Kenya found the going tough with regard to this matter. But never one to give up, Ndingi, who was at the forefront of the campaign against artificial methods of family planning continued to agitate against it. Population and development, Ndingi argued, taking a cue from the Vatican, were serious issues but they had to be seen within the context of the sacredness of human life and the dignity of the human person.

But the issue had taken a global dimension. The most powerful countries on earth backed the Cairo draft on population control and abortion and the Holy See saw that as the defeat of the family which it believed was the bedrock of the Church. Even before this, Ndingi had already taken the moral plane and started exhorting the youth on morality and family values. In an address to Moi University Catholic Students Association, the Archbishop impressed upon the youth to lead moral lives, "not as a law imposed from outside, but as one inscribed in heart and mind by the renewing action of the Holy Spirit."

The Archbishop's stance on condom use was uncompromising. Some people accused him of being too rigid on the Church's teachings on family planning. On October 11, 2003, Ndingi told BBC's Panorama programme that HIV/AIDS was spreading fast in Africa and in Kenya in particular because of the use of the condom.

"You give a Kenyan a condom and for him or her it's a licence to have intercourse," he said. "They think they are protected and they are not."

He shocked the host of the programme when he suggested that condoms should not be made at all and that the ban on their usage should also extend to non-Catholics. "The laws of God affect everybody," he said.

Throughout his days in Nairobi, the war on condoms was to preoccupy the Archbishop. The media made fun of him because of this but he did not seem to care one bit about what they were saying. The availability of condoms, he insisted at every opportunity, had created a free-for-all situation where the youth were engaging in sex at will.

# CHAPTER SEVENTEEN

## *Serving three Presidents*

One morning in 1971, Archbishop Ndingi left the bishop's house in Machakos. His destination was President Jomo Kenyatta's residence in Gatundu. Gatundu was a familiar place for Ndingi because he used to frequent the many dance events that Mzee Kenyatta was fond of hosting.

Accompanied by Fr George Muhoho who was Kenyatta's nephew, Ndingi would arrive at Gatundu, proceed to greet the old man who always responded with a rare enthusiasm.

"You are here, *Muthikabu*," he would welcome him. *Muthikabu* is a Kikuyu corruption of the Kiswahili word for bishop, *askofu*.

"Yes we have come," Ndingi would respond.

"Okay, welcome and make sure you have fun," Kenyatta would tell him and then continue to await the onset of the dances which he thoroughly enjoyed. The dances, which saw an ensemble of dancers drawn from diverse parts of the country would begin in the early afternoon and end at about 6.30 p.m.

On this day, however, Ndingi was not there for the dances. He wanted to see Kenyatta on another matter. He wanted some financial assistance for his diocese in Machakos. One of the parishes was seriously in need of a church. After the usual welcome, Ndingi proceeded to table his problems.

"Mzee, I have a small problem," he told the president.

"What is it, *Muthikabu*?" Kenyatta asked.

Ndingi explained that he needed some money to construct a church and wondered if the president would look kindly on his request.

Kenyatta listened, all the while playing about with his flywhisk. After a while, he told Ndingi. "*Muthikabu*, this house belongs to two people," he said, "and decisions must be taken by both. Would you please excuse me?"

Kenyatta walked out, all the while calling out Mama Ngina's name. He must have gone to consult. Kenyatta was a family man and could not do any thing pertaining to the family without consulting his wife. After a while, he came back.

"Here," he told the bishop, "this small token will help you."

It was five thousand shillings, a hefty amount at the time. It is this money that Ndingi used to put up a church in Mitaboni, Machakos.

Later when Ndingi set up a school in Rongai, Nakuru, he met Kenyatta who had heard about the school. Ndingi had another small request. He wanted a bigger piece of land because the land on which the school was built was small. Again, Kenyatta listened and told him,

"You have done your part. Let me know whatever you need."

Ndingi drew up a long list of his requirements and sent it to State House. Kenyatta never responded.

"I suspect he did not get the letter," Ndingi now says, "It was not like him to ignore things that way."

But much later, Kenyatta donated a large piece of land to a Catholic institution in Nakuru to set up its own structures.

In many ways, Ndingi's relationship with Kenyatta was quite

cordial. But the archbishop says that Kenyatta had a special way of dealing with the clergy.

"I never heard him talk about a clergyman, whatever his denomination, in a negative way. He tried to see the positive things in the clergy," Ndingi says.

Equally interesting was Ndingi's relationship with former president Moi. He was a fierce critic of the Moi regime in his years in Nakuru, especially in relation to the clashes and the early years in Nairobi. One would have expected his relationship with Moi to be irretrievably damaged. But was it? Moi and Ndingi seemed to enjoy some inscrutable harmony which was, in all respects, beyond the ken of those who knew the two men. In almost all cases when Ndingi called on Moi, the president was ready to listen.

Moi would refer to the archbishop as 'bishop' and he had respect for him that few others could understand. On matters of development, the two men moved in perfect tandem. "Former President Moi, always gave me an appointment when I had issues to address with him. He never refused to see me," Ndingi recalls.

In spite of what was seemingly going on between the two men, played out most vividly in the media, Ndingi believes that Moi was a blessing to him in many ways. "It was through him that we were able to develop Baringo and East Pokot," he says, "Moi was fully behind us on this."

At one time, Ndingi remembers talking to Moi about the problems of Baringo and Moi was forthright;

"What do you require, Bishop?" he asked him.

"Your Excellency, we require three things: roads, hospitals and water," he responded.

Moi assured him that all would be done. "Just call upon me whenever you require my help."

From then onwards, the entire provincial administration was behind him. At one time, bulldozers were digging up the roads as Ndingi's convoy, taking provisions into the heart of East Pokot, waited for the roads to be cleared. This was an indication that the president had honoured his promise and at a great speed.

At no time did Moi decline to see the archbishop when he needed to. "He always granted me appointments at short notice," he recalls, "and he took a keen interest in what we were doing." Moi remained a part of Ndingi's working group in the larger Baringo. Even when they differed, Moi was willing to help. Whenever they met, he always asked him, "what can I do for you, Bishop?"

On matters of development and sincerity, Moi believed in Ndingi. There were those around him who might have tried to convince him that Ndingi did not mean very well for the government on account of his frequent pronouncements against social injustice and human rights violation but Moi apparently paid no heed to them. That could be the reason he appointed him to a presidential working committee in the 1980s. It is instructive that this was at a time when Ndingi was at his most rabid self in Nakuru.

At around this time, Ndingi spent a lot of time going round the country with the presidential committee gathering views from a cross section of Kenyans. Then he would go ballistic the following day whenever the government was caught up in a case of social injustice.

"But Moi knew I did not mean ill and I knew he did not have bad intentions for me," he says.

Under Kibaki, things were slightly different. Kibaki came to power when Ndingi was entering his final phase of active episcopacy. He had been at the helm of the archdiocese for over six years during which time he appeared to have somewhat mellowed.

Ndingi first met Kibaki when he was the Bishop of Machakos in the 1970s. At that time, the man who would be president was attending a ceremony in which a nun from Nyeri was to take her final vows. Kibaki was MP for Bahati at the time.

The first thing to strike Ndingi about Kibaki was that he did not talk much but he listened a lot. "He was of a quiet temperament though he seemed to act swiftly," he recalls.

Kibaki engaged Ndingi in a brief conversation. He wanted to know what nuns actually did in their calling. "What do the Sisters do?" he inquired, "What is their main work?"

He explained that they could work anywhere, in the education sector, in the health sector and in catechetical work. All the while, Kibaki was just nodding and absorbing what Ndingi was saying.

When Kibaki became president, Ndingi met him a number of times when he attended Mass at the Holy Family Basilica, the seat of the Archbishop of Nairobi. Ndingi discovered how difficult it was to get in touch with Kibaki in the year 2005 when he desperately wanted to meet the president to discuss what he calls an issue of grave national importance.

The president's men wanted to know what it was that Ndingi wanted to tell the president, but the archbishop would not budge.

"I told them I had to speak to the president and no one else," he recalls, "they insisted that they had to know what I wanted to tell him."

For a while, State House and the archbishop would not budge. Ndingi held his ground insisting that he was not asking for a favour but that it was in the interest of the nation that he needed to see the president. It took a month before the State House Comptroller granted him an interview.

At State House, Kibaki listened calmly to what the archbishop had to say. At the end of the encounter, the president looked at Ndingi and said, *"Mzuri sana hiyo"* (that is very good). Nothing surprising because that is what the president was wont to say. But he promised to act on what the archbishop had told him. According to Ndingi, the first issue he wanted acted on was swiftly dealt with. The other one had to wait for six months.

Ndingi recalls that Kibaki struck him as an intellectual and a keen listener, but what he liked most was that the president listened to him and acted on what he had to tell him immediately.

He would have wanted to interact with the president much more but both seemed too busy for such social moments. When they, however, got to talking, each lent the other the ear patiently.

After Ndingi's retirement, Kibaki, like Moi before him, appointed Ndingi the chairman of the Resettlement Committee of the Internally Displaced People. In his new role, the Emeritus Bishop of Nairobi started crusading for peace alongside ensuring that the resettlement programme worked.

"President Kibaki and ODM leader, Hon. Raila Odinga, should make sure all Kenyans are safe. Why are people who have lived as brothers, sisters and neighbours killing each other? Is there any need to fight over poll results?" Ndingi posed.

Ndingi believed that the strict separation of religion and State does not mean the exclusion of religion and reason from democratic deliberation. Church leaders must critique State policy on religious grounds, lobby for change relying on religious authority, and leaders should never fuse civil and religious authority.

## Missing the hat

On October 6, 2007, Archbishop Raphael Ndingi Mwana 'a Nzeki retired as the primate of the Nairobi archdiocese. He had earlier written to the Vatican on attaining the age of seventy-five asking to retire. It is usually a requirement of the Canon Law (No 401) that on attaining seventy-five years of age, a bishop notifies the Vatican after which the Holy See names a successor.

The Holy See might choose to decline the resignation and ask the bishop to continue. In some cases, the Vatican might take years in naming a successor or effecting the retirement meaning that the bishop stays in office until told to officially retire by the Vatican. In fact, the law in question states:

> A diocesan bishop who has completed his seventy-fifth year of age is requested to offer his resignation from office to the supreme Pontiff, who, taking all the circumstances into account, will make provision accordingly.

In the case of Ndingi, a number of months elapsed between the time he wrote the resignation letter and the time the Vatican accepted it and named a successor.

So when Archbishop John Njue was appointed the new Ordinary for the Nairobi Metropolitan Archdiocese, it did not surprise many. Since Ndingi announced that he had officially written his resignation letter, in January 2007, many Christians expected him to retire any time.

He also did not know the exact date when the Vatican would ask him to retire; "I will continue serving you as I wait to hear from the Holy Father," he told Christians when he broke news about his retirement.

When the Vatican announced Njue's appointment on

October 5, it was the end of Archbishop Ndingi's active life in the episcopacy. Many were sad to see him go after nearly forty years of service. But many wondered if Ndingi would really go "quietly into that dark night" of retirement. Would his voice finally be stilled by the placidity of retirement or would he continue rumbling in the jungles of repose in keeping with the characteristics many people had come to know?

When he delivered his final farewell in November 2007 at the Holy Family Basilica, there were tears for his departure. He called on the Christians to pray for him in his retirement and on an apocalyptic note, asked them to "reflect and re-examine their lives in their sojourn on Earth."

"As a retiree," he said, "I plead for your prayers while I ask God to forgive me for any sin I may have committed while in office."

The man who many acknowledge was a thoroughly organised prelate must have had clear plans for his retirement. But no, he did not have any. Apparently, he had immersed himself into his work so much that he forgot to plan for his retirement. Ndingi did not even have a clear idea about his retirement home. But he somehow had faith that he would eventually have some abode to retire to.

"At the moment, I have no plans for my retirement," he told reporters, "I will rest for a year or so and then I will be available to all who need my services."

With that, Ndingi retired to a quiet residence in Lavington where, at the time the book was being written, he was residing with the Holy Ghost Fathers most of whom he had known all the days of his priesthood.

According to the Canon Law (402), a bishop whose resignation has been accepted acquires the title "emeritus" of his diocese. Thus Ndingi acquired the title, "Emeritus Archbishop of Nairobi" to begin his time of rest from active service.

But if he thought he would spend at least a year in retirement before bouncing back into public life, other people had other plans for him. Following the post-election chaos that erupted in 2008 and which led to the displacement of hundreds of thousands of people especially in Rift valley, Ndingi's services were in urgent demand.

In April, 2008, President Kibaki appointed the retired archbishop the chairman of the Committee for the Resettlement of the Internally Displaced Persons. The most enduring picture was of Ndingi and President Kibaki raising hundreds of millions of shillings in Nairobi in May of the same year and of him seating with other dignitaries at scores of peace meetings attended by the country's political leaders.

All of a sudden, the man who had thought he would spend at least one year in retirement was back in circulation visiting Internally Displaced People's camps and chairing meetings beyond the confines of the city.

One question that many kept asking upon the retirement of Ndingi and the elevation of his successor to cardinal was: why was Ndingi never made cardinal?

Though the reporters were never that blunt, always couching the question along the lines, "do you think Kenya is likely to get a cardinal soon?," they expected that Ndingi, being the head of the country's most geographically important archdiocese would be given the red hat.

Ndingi would always say, "It is the prerogative of the Holy Father to appoint whoever he so wishes." Those who were close to Ndingi say that at no time did he entertain the thought that he would be made cardinal. Ndingi was about seventy when

Cardinal Otunga died and threw open the position of cardinal in the country. There was the argument that even in retirement, Otunga was still a cardinal and eligible to participate in a papal election should a conclave arise. There was hence not a great likelihood that another cardinal would be appointed in Otunga's lifetime. The question of age may have worked against Ndingi somewhat and some saw it as a big disappointment for him to have missed the hat.

Speculation after speculation as to why he missed the cardinal's hat swirled around. But Ndingi did not appear bothered by that. A few years after the death of Otunga and when it became clear that the Vatican was not in a hurry to name a cardinal for Kenya in spite of the fact that Pope John Paul II held a final consistory before he died in 2005, Ndingi might have accepted that he probably was not going to be a likely candidate for the coveted red hat. He went on with his work undeterred even as the gap left by Otunga yawned ever the more.

As Ndingi went into retirement there was ambivalence as to what kind of man had retired. Some felt that the Ndingi of Nakuru was not the same man as the Archbishop of Nairobi who had just retired. Others felt that he had sold out to the system and that that was why his criticism of the Kibaki regime was somewhat tempered. Still, there are those who saw in the man a consistency that he had carried throughout his episcopacy. Even as he appeared muted, he still was not afraid of speaking his mind on controversial issues. He still tore into politicians when he thought they were wrong regardless of whether they were in government or in opposition. With regard to the government, there was no knowing on which side Ndingi would fall.

"He blew hot and cold," said one politician. But those who knew him also knew that he did no such thing. "He fell on the side of justice," they said, regardless of what others thought.

One of the most coruscating criticisms of the bishop was during the constitutional referendum of 2005, when he shied away from telling his Catholic flock how to vote. Despite calls for the Church to chart the way, Ndingi as the primate of the biggest metropolitan See and therefore one who would, one might presume, be listened to more, refused to tell his flock whether to vote Yes or No.

Was he wise in doing so? Some thought he was. And those who thought this way were vindicated by what happened shortly after Ndingi retired and John Cardinal Njue came in. Njue is as outspoken as Ndingi and he plunged headlong into the *majimbo* debate which was, at the time, shaping the political discourse in the 2007 presidential campaigns.

The opposition was widely seen to be rooting for the majimbo system of government. The incumbent government's side was an emphatic no; *majimbo* would balkanise the country. Njue sought to advise his flock: "*Majimbo* is dangerous for the country," he said, "people must reject it."

A can of worms exploded. Njue's statement was seen as signaling the Catholic Church's tacit support for the government. Njue was accused of taking sides, he was traduced, he was pummelled, he was called names in various hate-spewing websites. It did not help matters that Njue belonged to a community that was seen to be firmly behind President Kibaki.

Questions still abound as to whether Njue would have met with the same criticism had he advised otherwise. But chances were that any which way he advised, one side was certain to take offence.

In retrospect, had Ndingi given his flock the so-called "spiritual direction" on how to vote during the referendum,

## A Voice Unstilled

he probably would have faced a barrage of accusations, his objectivity impugned and his non-partisanship called into question. The jury is still out on whether he acted wisely on this. Whether it was an act of judiciousness or cowardice as some claimed, Ndingi chose to reserve his comment on this matter.

On the day the Archdiocese of Nairobi held a farewell Mass for him on August 16, 2008, a number of articles appeared in the media hailing Ndingi's fearlessness in the fight against social injustice. A few days later a columnist wrote a rustic article claiming that "Ndingi was anything but fearless." The article claimed that the archbishop's episcopacy was not marked by any remarkable traits of courage and that his fight for social justice was lukewarm. The fact that he also never told his flock how to vote was cited as an example of the archbishop's cowardice.

But on August 22, another article headlined "How can a man be so wrong about Ndingi"[1] outlined the many examples of courage the archbishop had shown.

Such were the emotions Ndingi evoked. There were those who probably never liked him; there were those who liked him but there were few who could ignore him.

---

[1] *The standard*, August 22, 2008

# Epilogue

On December 25, 2006, Archbishop Ndingi turned seventy-five. This is the age at which Catholic bishops are supposed to retire. As required in the Canon Law, a bishop is supposed to write to the Vatican notifying the Pope that he had reached retirement age. Ndingi duly wrote the letter but he intimated that he was willing to serve until the Holy Father gave directions on the matter. In some cases, the Pope can choose to keep a bishop who has reached retirement age for a number of years before appointing a successor.

In Ndingi's case, it took almost a year before the Pope accepted his resignation on October 6, 2007 and appointed Archbishop John Njue, the then Coadjutor Archbishop of Nyeri and chairman of the Kenya Episcopal Conference as his successor.

In what to many people came as a surprise, the Pope shortly afterwards announced that Njue was to be installed cardinal, becoming the second Kenyan cardinal after the late Maurice Michael Otunga.

Njue had been appointed the Coadjutor of the Nyeri Diocese at a time when the archbishop of the diocese, Nicodemus Kirima was gravely ill. He had been expected to take over the diocese upon his demise.

On November 1, 2007, the day Njue was installed as the Archbishop of Nairobi at the Holy Family Basilica, Archbishop Kirima who was present at the installation and who had seemingly recovered well enough to continue with his apostolic duties was taken ill. He never sat through the ceremony to the end, and he never recovered. He died a few days later.

On March 2, 2008, Urbanus Kioko, Bishop Emeritus of Machakos and who took over from Ndingi passed away. Ndingi was in great sorrow for a man with whom he had travelled a long journey.

On July, 20 2008, Ndingi celebrated his farewell Mass at colourful ceremony at the Holy Family Basilica. That day, all the major daily newspapers had lengthy articles extolling the character of the bishop who had just retired. The following week, many more articles were to follow, some criticized the archbishop for having been too cosy with the government after his posting to Nairobi. One particular article was headlined "Ndingi was anything but fearless." The writer detailed how the bishop had sold out to the ruling class and how he had inexplicably changed after he came from Nakuru. But other writers chimed in, supporting the bishop and calling him a defender of the common man's rights. It was clear that, for some time to come, Ndingi would still be a figure who elicited varied reactions amongst the people of Kenya even as he headed for his retirement.

But soon after his retirement, President Mwai Kibaki appointed Ndingi the chairman of the advisory board of the Humanitarian Fund for Victims of Post-election Violence, ensuring once again that this trenchant voice and colourful character would not go quietly into the dark night. In this capacity he continued to make news, often being photographed with the politicians at IDP camps and travelling from Nairobi to Rift Valley to ensure that the IDPs were resettled.

Incidentally after retirement, Ndingi went to live with the Holy Ghost Fathers in Lavington as his retirement house, which the diocese had purchased for him awaited completion. For those

## Epilogue

who might have misunderstood the man's relationship with the white fathers, this was an oddity. But those who knew that his relationship with the white priests with whom he had had a few in his apostolic career was quite sound, were not surprised.

In 2008, Ndingi's house was finally completed and he moved in to continue with his retirement in the serenity of the suburbs of Nairobi.

## LIST OF LATIN TERMS USED

"*eos libere nominat Pontifex Romanus* - the Pope freely nominates bishops.
*Ad limina* – the five-yearly visits to Rome made by bishops.
*Defensor civitatis* - the defender of the city.
*Defensor populi* - the defender of the people.
*e' páter les Bourgeois* – shocking the established system, doing things out of the norm
*IInstrumentum Laboris* - the working document of the synod.
*Propaganda Fide* – the congregation for the evangelization of people.
*Secundum mentem ecclesiae* - according to the mind of the Church.
*The lineamenta* - outline document of the synod.
*The terna* - A list of three candidates to be consecrated bishop prepared for the Pope by the Nuncio.

## Pictorial Appendix

In Junior seminary, Kilimambogo in 1952. Ndingi is the first right.

Deacon Ndingi with his colleagues soon after his Diaconate Ordination

## Pictorial Appendix

Ndingi on his way to Tom Mboya's wedding at St Peter's Clavers.

In 1969 at John Fisher College with Bishop Fulton

As a young priest, Ndingi blesses his parents.

Ndingi with his brother

## Pictorial Appendix

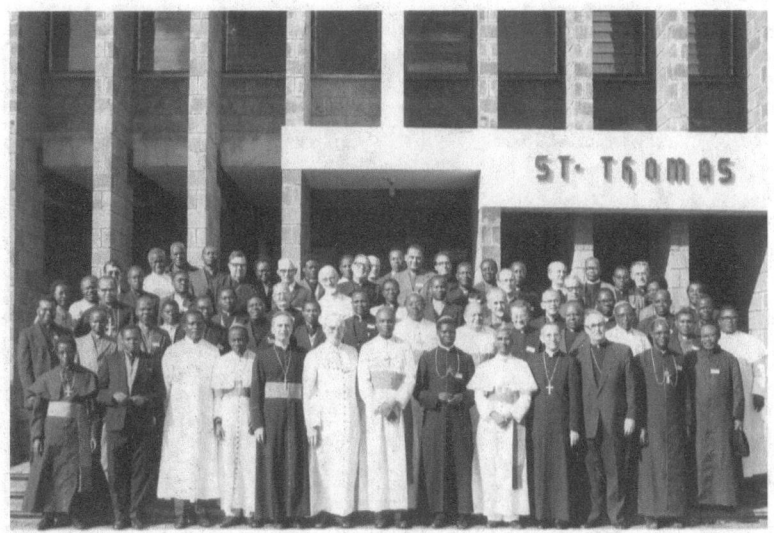

At a bishops and priests meeting at St Thomas Aquinas Major Seminary

Ndingi with his mother two weeks before she passed on.

## Pictorial Appendix

During his installation as Bishop of Machakos

Young priest Ndingi blessing the faithful after his ordination.

## Pictorial Appendix

Ndingi with other bishops at the Holy Family Basilica when the late Pope John Paul II visited Kenya.

Ndingi, with former president Moi, after Mass at the Holy Family Basilica.

Ndingi with Archbishop J.J Mcarthy in 1968, in Rocherter.

## Pictorial Appendix

At the Holy Family Basilica

Giving a keen ear to Pope John Paul II in Rome

## Pictorial Appendix

Ndingi sharing with the late Pope John Paul II

Blessing of Taiti mission in Baringo District, Nakuru Diocese

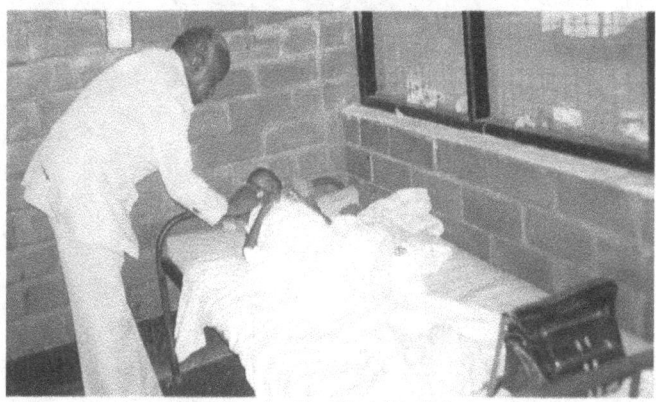
Ndingi visits the sick at Kibwezi Health Centre

# INDEX

## A
African Inland Church 16
African Synod 169, 176
Alexander Muge 128, 129
AMECEA 89, 185
Amnesty International 124
Apostolic Administrator 67
Apostolic Nunciature 153
Apostolic Nuncio 34
Archbishop Ceasar Gatimu 41, 62
Archbishop Emmanuel Milingo 57
Archbishop J.J. McCarthy 2, 18, 26, 27, 33, 34, 42, 44, 53, 55, 58, 62
Archbishop John J. Foley 97
Archbishop John Njenga vi, vii, 5, 20, 31, 33, 41, 102, 107, 108, 109, 152
Archbishop John Njue 107, 203, 207, 209
Archbishop Nicodemus Kirima vii, 54, 55, 209
Archbishop of Krakow 156
Archbishop of Paris 159
Archbishop of Westminster 159
Archbishop Okoth 107, 109, 115
Archbishop Perluigi Sartorelli 66, 67
Archbishop Stephen Ondiek 91
Asumbi Teacher's College 102, 193
Attorney General 123

## B
Bahati Parish 141
Beecher Report of 1949 77
Bishop Alexander Kipsang Muge 84
Bishop Cornelius Korir 79, 107
Bishop Gatimu Ngandu Girls 36
Bishop Langford Smith 70
Bishop Willigers 71, 72
Bishop's House 114
British Refugee Council 124
Bull of Erection 73

## C
Cambridge School Certificate 29
Canon Law 170, 174, 177, 209
Cardinal Agosto Casaroli 97
Cardinal Jaime Sin 166
Cardinal Stefan Wyszynsnki 159
Catholic Ordinaries 48
Catholic University of Eastern Africa 175
Charles Njonjo 63
Church of Rome 138
Church Province of Kenya 73, 88

1917 Code of Cannon Law 156
Commission on Africanisation 82
Common Entrance Examination 15
Congregation of Bishops 157, 158
Congregation for the Evangelisation 72
Congregation for Divine Worship 174
Consolata Fathers 36
Convent of Our Lady of Lourdes 94
Criminal Investigation Department 118

## D
Daniel Arap Moi 85, 96, 166, 167, 199, 200
Daniel Munuve 14
Democratic Party 126
Diocese of Eldoret 75
Diocese of Jinja 71
Diocese of Kitui 94
Director of Gatechetics 78
Dr E.F Schumacher 193
Dr Henry Okullu 84, 128

## E
East Africa 34
Eldama Ravine 94
Elijah Mwangale 98
Emeritus Archbishop of Mombasa vi, 5
Emilio Njeru of Meru 41, 57
Episcopal Conferences of Africa 171
Etikoni 13

## F
Father Edward Fitz 9
Father George Gathongo 41
Father Komotho wa Njeri 41
Father Paul Njoroge Senior 41
Father Peter Mbuchi 184, 185, 186, 187, 188, 189, 190, 191
Feast of Saint Joseph 111
Fidei Donum Priests 81
FORD 104, 112, 132
Fr Anthony Prunty S.P.S 76
Fr Bobby Kavanagh 149
Fr Boran 43
Fr Brian Cunningham 140
Fr Brian Hearne 176, 177
Fr Cecily McGarry SJ 186, 190
Fr Christy Burke 95
Fr Dennis Newman viii, 138, 42, 76, 82, 141
Fr Eddie Lolar 100
Fr Edward Tieanan 61
Fr Finbar O' Sullivan 25

# Index

Fr Fintan Byre 82
Fr Francis Gichia 79
Fr Francis Mirango vii, 119, 142, 147, 148
Fr Frank Comerford 69
Fr George Muhoho 36, 55, 65, 197
Fr James Maloba viii
Fr Jeremiah Buckley 76
Fr Joachim Gitonga 63
Fr John Bergman 49
Fr John Jones S.P.S 76
Fr John O'Brien 147, 148
Fr John O'Meara 42, 45
Fr Josef Gasser 76
Fr Joseph M'lengera vii, 139, 141
Fr Lawrence Njoroge ix, 47
Fr Magee 137
Fr Maurice Lwanga 76
Fr McCauley 68
Fr Michael Dillon 141
Fr Michael O' Connor 29, 31
Fr Moses Muraya viii, 116, 144
Fr Ndikaru wa Teresia 94, 107, 119, 120, 121, 122, 163
Fr Noel Delaney 69
Fr Nuggent 25
Fr P.J. McCamphill vii
Fr Patrick Kanja Wachira v, viii, 79, 127, 129, 145, 117, 144
Fr Paul Wallace 17
Fr Peter Coyle 100
Fr Peter Kairo 76
Fr Peter Kimani vii
Fr Peter Mungai vii
Fr Remigio Dalsanto 184
Fr Romeo di Berti 76
Fr Sean Grogan 4, 5, 43, 44, 100
Fr Sean O'Laoire 100
Fr Thomas Kiggins 76
Fr Wilhelm Arap Sambu 79

G
Gatundu 197
General Service Unit 118
Gerry McCluskey 140
Giants Group 101
Giovanni Battista Montini, Archbishop of Milan 56

H
Hekima Jesuit School of Theology 180
Hezekiah Oyugi 100

Hinsley 48
Holy Family Basilica 32, 89, 210, 204
Holy Ghost Fathers 9, 47, 81, 210
Holy Ghost Missionaries 35, 57, 58, 59, 61
Holy Rosary Church 74
Holy See 195, 203
Holy Week 5
*Humanae Vitae* 192

I
Ignitian exercises 186
Inculturation 172, 176
Internally Displaced Persons 205, 210
IPPG 167
Ishmael Chelanga 116
Isaiah Mathenge 63
Isindore Onyango 54

J
J.M Kariuki 98
Jean-Marie Lustiger 159
Joe Lynch 32, 33
Jomo Kenyatta 84, 197, 198
Joseph Nzeki Ngila 10, 23, 24

K
Kabaa High School 35
Kabaa Mission 9, 12, 16, 25
Kalonzo Musyoka 168
KANU 46, 85, 86, 90, 91, 92, 93, 94, 96, 104, 105, 106, 107, 114, 119, 126,128, 166
Karol Wojytla 155, 156
Kel Chemicals 119
Kenya Broadcasting Corporation 30
Kenya Catholic Secretariat 108
Kenya Episcopal Conference vi, 63, 79, 88, 94, 115, 209
Kenya National Human Rights Commission 117
Kenya Times Tower 119
Khoja Mosque 30
Kibaki 200, 201, 202, 205, 207, 210
Kijana Wamalwa 132
Kilimambogo Seminary 17, 25
Kilimambogo Teachers Training College 18
Kiltegan 71, 75, 81
Kipkelion 104
Kiserian 3
Kokwet 105
Kombe 16

# Index

**L**
Lanet 73
*Lineamenta* 171, 172
Lions Club of Nakuru 101
Little Sisters Novitiate 82
Loretu Limuru 35, 51

**M**
Machakos v, 9, 26, 53, 58, 59, 60, 67, 72
Maina Kiai 117
Mama Ngina 198
Mangu High School 35
Maria Muthoki 10
Mary Gertrude Kasiva 189, 190
Masaku 9
Mau Mau 22
Maurice Cardinal Otunga 33, 99, 113, 153, 154, 155, 163, 206
Mbiuni 13
Medical Missionaries of Mary 77
Mill Hill Fathers 36, 37, 71, 76, 81
Milton Obote 71, 72
Minister for Basic Education 52
Minister for National Guidance and Political Affairs 92
Moi University Catholic Students Association 195
Molo 104, 107, 110
Moses Mudamba Mudavadi 46, 90
Mr Benedict Mailu 11
Mr Kenneth Matiba 166
Mr Kilovia 14
Mr Paul Ngei 65
Mr Philemon Mwaisaka 101
Mwangaza Spiritual Jesuit House 190
*Mwolyo* 15
Myanyani Primary School 11, 12

**N**
Nairobi Archdiocese 191
Nairobi National Park 4
Naivasha Catholic Church 75
Nakuru Diocese vii, 72
National Convention Executive Committee 166
National Council of Churches of Kenya 115
National Democractic Party 132
National Fascist Party 14
Native Schools Examiniation Board 50
Nditha 16
Ngili 15

Nyahururu 94

**O**
Obadiah Kariuki 64
Olengurueni 104
Ongata Rongai 4
Our Lady of Visitation, Makadara vi, 29, 55

**P**
Peace Commission 87
Pentecostal Church of East Africa 88
Peter Hebblethwaite 159, 175
Peter Kiarie Njoroge 36
Peter Okondo 128
Pius Katiku 14
Poland 156
Pontifical Council for Social Communications 97
Pope John Paul II 155, 170, 192
Pope John XXIII 56
Pope Paul VI 1, 56, 57, 135, 136, 178
Pope Pius XI 48
Precious Blood Riruta 36
Prefecture Apostolic of Kavirondo 75
Presbyterian Church of East Africa 81, 84
Prof John Mbithi 81, 108, 124, 125, 130
Prof Wangari Maathai 118, 120, 121, 122
Propaganda Fide 72

**Q**
Queen of Apostles Seminary vi, 34

**R**
Raila Odinga 202
Rev Timothy Njoya 84
Rome 135, 157, 158, 170
Rt Rev David Gitari 84
Ruaraka 34

**S**
Samson Mwangi viii
Second World War 13
Shariff Nassir 92
Simeon Matheka 13
Simon Ndile 14
Sister Angelina Mumbi viii
Sisters of St Joseph 77
St Augustine's 150
St John Fischer college 54
St John of the Cross 2
St Joseph's Seminary 80

# Index

St Mary's Nairobi 36
St Mary's Yala 36
St Mulumba Catholic Church 94
St Patrick's Catholic Church 94
St Patrick's Missionary Society 75, 76
St Paul's Catholic Chapel 94, 95
St Peter Clever's Catholic Church 29, 30, 32
St Theresa's Gekano Girl's Secondary School 94
St Thomas Aquinas Senior Seminary-Morogoro 19, 20, 27, 59, 182
State House 110, 202

## T
Tala 29
Tangaza College 179
The Archbishop of Dakar Senegal 173
*The Catholic Mirror* 69
Thomas More 159
Tom Mboya 61

## U
Ufungamano House 87
Uganda 1, 71, 72
Uganda Protectorate 75

Uhuru Park 119
United Nations 124
University of Nairobi vii, 87, 91, 95
Urbanus Kioko 18, 68, 210

## V
Vicariate of Kisumu 75
Vicariate of the Upper Nile 75

## W
Wanyoike wa Thungu 63
*Weekly Review* 88
West Pokot 141
White Highlands 3
World Conference on Population and Development in Cairo 195

## Y
Yatta 65
Young Christian Students Organisation 79

## Z
Zanzibar 34

www.ingramcontent.com/pod-product-compliance
Lightning Source LLC
Chambersburg PA
CBHW011744290426
44113CB00017BA/2645